Who Is My Self?

# Who Is My Self?

## A Guide to Buddhist Meditation

The Poṭṭhapāda Sutta
The Buddha's Words on Self and Consciousness
Interpreted and Explained

by

# AYYA KHEMA

WISDOM PUBLICATIONS · BOSTON

WISDOM PUBLICATIONS
199 ELM STREET
SOMERVILLE, MASSACHUSETTS 02144

*Library of Congress Cataloging-in-Publication Data*

Khema, Ayya.
Who is my self? : a guide to Buddhist meditation / Ayya Khema.
p.    cm.
ISBN 0-86171-127-0 (alk. paper)
1. Tipiṭaka. Suttapiṭaka. Dīghanikāya. Poṭṭhapādasutta—Criticism,
interpretation, etc.    2. Meditation—Buddhism.
I. Title.
BQ1300.P685K54  1997
294.3'823—DC21                                                                97–2606


ISBN  0-86171-127-0


02  01  00  99
6    5    4    3


*Designed by:* L·J·SAWLiT & Adie Russell


Wisdom Publications' books are printed on acid-free paper and meet the guidelines for the
permanence and durability of the Committee on Production Guidelines for
Book Longevity of the Council on Library Resources.

Printed in the United States of America

# Contents

# Publisher's Acknowledgment

The publisher gratefully acknowledges the generous support of the Hershey Family Foundation in sponsoring the production of this book.

# Preface

It seems we have come to a time in the history of humankind when more and more people are searching for life's meaning. In the past, family life, religion, political affiliations, and/or specific occupations were thought to be sufficient to satisfy human yearning for fulfillment. Although this longing is mostly unacknowledged and seldom verbalized, it exists in the heart of every person.

Today many of the former preoccupations, while still being used, no longer provide a firm basis for a meaningful life. However, if we think that twentieth-century humanity is unique in this search for meaning, we will soon know otherwise when we read the Buddha's discourse on the following pages.

Here a wanderer named Poṭṭhapāda asks the Buddha innumerable questions about self and consciousness, and the Buddha patiently and painstakingly answers him with exact guidelines for establishing himself on the spiritual path and reaching final perfection. This took place two thousand five hundred years ago, but is just as pertinent for us today as it was then.

We will also find that friends and companions of Poṭṭhapāda are not in agreement with this new way of thinking and try to persuade him to relinquish his interest in the Buddha's teaching. This too is not unknown in our day and age.

I hope that, with the explanations and interpretations given, the Discourse will come to life for the reader and will help to show the direction in which life's meaning can be found—namely, in our spiritual evolution. Anyone who finds inner peace, happiness, and fulfillment contributes to the peace and happiness of the world.

_____

This book contains the taped talks given during a three-week meditation course held at the Buddhist meditation center Land of Medicine Buddha in Soquel, California, during May and June 1994.

Due to the kindness, generosity, and commitment of Gail Gokey and Alicia Yerburgh, we now have the text before us that can serve as a support for practice.

I am personally deeply grateful to Gail and Alicia for this work done with love, and to Toni Stevens, who organized and managed the retreat with great skill. My gratitude also goes to Traudel Reiss, whose computer expertise made all corrections possible.

Wisdom Publications, under the able guidance of Tim McNeill, provides a wonderful outlet for the Buddha's teaching, and I am happy to be numbered among their authors.

If those who read this book gain more faith in the Buddha's teaching, more love for the practice, or more insight into absolute truth, all of us who worked on this book will feel immensely gratified, as well as encouraged to give our time and love again in a similar way.

May this book be a companion in the search for humanity's highest potential, which all of us carry within as the seed of enlightenment.

May the Dhamma live in many hearts.

*Ayya Khema*
*Buddha-Haus, Germany*
*1 July 1996*

# 1

## The Beginning:
## Morality

In the Theravādan tradition, we use the Pali Canon as our foundation for the words of the Buddha. Pali was the language spoken by the Buddha and is a derivative of Sanskrit. The difference between the two is similar to the difference between Latin and Italian. Sanskrit was spoken by learned scholars, and Pali, or a dialect akin to it, was spoken by ordinary folk. This teaching is grounded in a tradition that is two thousand five hundred years old.

The Pali Canon is also called the *Tipiṭaka*. *Ti* means "three" and *piṭaka* means "basket." The Three Baskets are the *Vinaya*, the rules and discipline for monks and nuns; the *Suttas*, the Buddha's discourses; and the *Abhidhamma*, the higher philosophy of the teaching. The reason for the name is that the *Tipiṭaka* was first written down on dried banana palm, or "ola" leaves. When dried, they become brittle but are still reasonably solid. Using a stylo, which resembles a screwdriver with a very fine point, the letters of the text were scratched into the ola leaves. Then the juice of a particular kind of berry was rubbed over the leaf and the excess removed; the dark indentation of the letters remained. This same process is still used in Sri Lanka to this day, where a certain monastery always keeps a set of the entire *Tipiṭaka*, handwritten on ola leaves. The monks repeatedly copy the texts from old leaves onto new ones, as the old ones decay. The leaves are held together with a heavy wood binding at top and bottom, and the parts are laced together. Should there be a donor, the wooden top-piece is often decorated with gold or silver in honor of the Buddha's words. These are not books as we know them and cannot be carried in one's hand or under the arm. Originally they were put into three baskets which were then carried around. This is how the Pali Canon was named the *Tipiṭaka*, or Three Baskets.

Throughout this book we shall be using an excellent English translation of the *Long Discourses of the Buddha*, the *Digha Nikāya*.[1] *Nikāya* means "collection" and *digha* means "long." Many years after his death, the Buddha's discourses were divided into five collections: the *Majjhima Nikāya*, Medium-Length Sayings; the *Digha Nikāya*, the Long Collection; the *Anguttara Nikāya*, a numerical assembly; the *Samyutta Nikāya*, a thematic collection; and the *Khuddaka Nikāya*, which contains everything that did not fit into the first four. These divisions were established simply as an aid to memory.

One reason why the *Digha Nikāya* is particularly interesting is that it contains suttas that give us the complete way of practice. We must remember that the Buddha taught on two levels: that of relative truth and that of absolute truth. When we first come into contact with the teachings, we have no idea what absolute truth is, and when we encounter some part of it, our minds boggle at it. Whatever questions we may ask will not be pertinent because we ask them on the level of relative truth and might have to be answered on the level of absolute truth. For example, we may have heard a Zen *koan* and thought, "What could that possibly mean? It's nonsense." But a *koan* can only be grasped from the standpoint of absolute truth. With that in mind, the meaning is always the same—that there is nothing and nobody there. We can also compare the two levels to the way we speak of familiar objects, such as a table or chair, and the way a physicist might describe them. To us these are pieces of furniture we can use. To the physicist they do not exist as such because the physicist knows they are only particles of matter and energy. Yet that same physicist will go home after work and sit down in a chair and use a table. When the Buddha teaches that there is nothing and nobody there, he is speaking on the level of absolute truth. On that level, our everyday world is an optical and mental illusion. That is the absolute truth. But the Buddha also taught on the relative level. He used words and concepts such as I, me, mine, you. He talked about all the things that concern us, such as *karma*, the purification of mind and emotions, and mind and body as we know them. We always need to remember that these two very different levels never operate together.

As we go through this particular discourse, we will find how to draw nearer to absolute truth. This is of great importance, for the Buddha promises that once we have realized absolute truth in ourselves, we will be permanently free from *dukkha* (suffering). The methods and guidelines that the Buddha gives us enable us to go step by step toward an immense and extraordinary realization, which was his own enlightenment experience. Today's science supports this experience, but it is better put the other way around—the words of the Buddha support today's science. Most of our scientists are not enlightened beings, although they know the truth that the universe consists of nothing but particles that come together and fall apart. Yet they have not realized that the one who knows, is exactly the same. If they had included themselves in their observations, these scientists would have been enlightened long ago and very probably teaching enlightenment rather than physics! We may have read or heard of all these things, we may be greatly interested in them, but without knowing how to proceed, this will be of little use to us. The great boon of the Buddha's teaching is that he gives us practical, step-by-step advice on how to follow the path.

The sutta I have chosen is known as the *Poṭṭhapāda Sutta*. Many of the suttas are named after the person to whom the Buddha was speaking and whose questions he was answering. This sutta is subtitled "States of Consciousness."

Most suttas start with the phrase "Thus have I heard," in Pali, *evam me suttam*, and the reason for this is that they were recited. At the Great Council of *Arahants* three months after the death of the Buddha, the recitation of each sutta contained information on where it had been taught, who was present, and a description of the prevailing situation. All this was included, so that the listening monks would be reminded of the occasion and would be able to agree or disagree with that particular oral transmission, and if necessary could suggest changes.

> Thus have I heard. Once the Lord was staying at Sāvatthi, in Jeta's Grove, in Anāthapiṇḍika's Park.

Anathapindika was a very rich merchant. When he heard the Buddha speak he was immediately fascinated and convinced. He decided to buy a monastery for the Buddha and his disciples, who up to that time had been wanderers. He found a beautiful mango grove, which belonged to a Prince Jeta. The prince, however, refused to sell. Anathapindika persisted, returning a second and third time to ask if he might purchase it. Finally, the prince told him that he could have it if he covered every inch of ground with gold coins. Anathapindika ordered his servants to bring barrels of gold coins and lay them down on the surface of the mango grove. The story goes that he ran out of coins while there was still one small area left uncovered, and when he told Prince Jeta of this, the prince agreed to give him this piece as a discount. To purchase the mango grove took one-third of Anathapindika's fortune. He spent another third on building and furnishing huts—though furniture in those days was simply some hooks on the walls, candles, and a hay-filled sack for a bed. The Buddha passed twenty-five "rain retreats" at Anathapindika's monastery. The rains retreat takes place during the three months of the rainy season in India. It is a time when monks and nuns are instructed to stay within their monasteries to study and meditate. The tradition came about because in the Buddha's time, all monks and nuns went on alms rounds to get their food. During the rainy season the small rice plants are transplanted in water and are quite hidden. The farmers complained to the Buddha that the monks and nuns trampled on their rice plants, and, as there were thousands of monks and nuns, this could result in a famine. The Buddha then decreed the rains retreat, during which time devoted disciples could bring food to the monasteries. The practice is observed to this day.

> And at that time the wanderer Poṭṭhapāda was at the debating-hall near the Tinduka tree, in the single-halled park of Queen Mallikā, with a large crowd of about three hundred wanderers.

A monk from a different tradition was often referred to in the suttas simply as a wanderer or ascetic. Queen Mallikā, who had apparently offered this hall to the wanderers, was the wife of King Pasenadi, and both were devoted followers of the Buddha.

> Then the Lord, rising early, took his robe and bowl and went to Sāvatthi for alms. But it occurred to him: "It is too early to go to Sāvatthi for alms. Suppose I were to go to the debating-hall to see the wanderer Poṭṭhapāda?" And he did so.

It was too early to go for alms because the people would not have the food prepared yet. Sāvatthi is often mentioned in the suttas because the monastery donated by Anathapindika was in that vicinity. Though the Buddha taught only in the north of India, his teaching has since spread to numerous other countries throughout Asia and is being established in Europe, the United States, Australia, and New Zealand.

> There Poṭṭhapāda was sitting with his crowd of wanderers, all shouting and making a great commotion, indulging in various kinds of unedifying conversation....

Now follow all the topics that are not worthy subjects for spiritual seekers: "such as about kings, robbers, ministers..."—politics, in other words, which usually creates divisive opinions; "armies, dangers, wars...";—gruesome and cruel events that burden the mind; "food, drink..."—which could foster sensual desire; "clothes, beds, garlands, perfumes..."—personal decorations to enhance one's appearance, while beds might convey the idea of sex; "relatives, carriages, villages, towns and cities, countries..."—such conversation would not be inspiring or uplifting, and would support attachment and identification. "[W]omen..."—these were all celibate monks, whose minds should not grasp at any features of the opposite sex. For nuns the converse would have applied. "[H]eroes..."—perhaps for us it would be pop-stars! "[S]treet and well gossip..."—even today, in so-called third-world coun- tries, the well is an important meeting place. Houses have no running water, so neighbors meet at the well and exchange all the latest news and gossip, which often results in backbiting or defamation. "[T]alk of the departed, desultory chat, speculations about land and sea, talk of being and nonbeing..."—these are all topics that, according to the Buddha, should be avoided. They do not bring deep understanding or turn the mind to practice, and have a distracting influence. This list of specific topics has been inserted into the sutta, and the text does not specify which of these the wanderers were discussing. It merely states that they were indulging in unsuitable conversation.

> But Poṭṭhapāda saw the Lord coming from a distance, and so he called his followers to order, saying: "Be quiet, gentlemen, don't make a noise, gentlemen! That ascetic Gotama is coming,

and he likes quiet and speaks in praise of quiet. If he sees that this company is quiet, he will most likely want to come and visit us." At this the wanderers fell silent.

Clearly Poṭṭhapāda was keen that the Buddha should come to see them, and he voices how pleased he is in the next paragraph.

> Then the Lord came to Poṭṭhapāda, who said: "Come, reverend Lord, welcome, reverend Lord! At last the reverend Lord has gone out of his way to come here. Be seated, Lord, a seat is prepared."
> The Lord sat down on the prepared seat, and Poṭṭhapāda took a low stool and sat down to one side. The Lord said: "Poṭṭhapāda, what were you all talking about? What conversation have I interrupted?"

The Buddha wanted to know their concerns, so he could help them with any questions.

> Poṭṭhapāda replied: "Lord, never mind the conversation we were having just now, it will not be difficult for the Lord to hear about that later."

He does not want to tell the Buddha what they were talking about because he wants an explanation of something far more important.

> In the past few days, Lord, the discussion among the ascetics and Brahmins of various schools, sitting together and meeting in the debating hall, has concerned the higher extinction of consciousness, and how this takes place.

This higher extinction of consciousness is *nirodha*. It is sometimes referred to as the ninth jhāna, which is the cessation of feeling and perception. (We shall be looking closely at the jhānas in later chapters.) Poṭṭhapāda is interested in this topic because in India at that time it was believed to be the highest possible state that could be reached on the spiritual path. In Pali, it is called *abhisaññānirodha*. *Abi* means "higher," *saññā* means "perception," and *nirodha* is the description of these concentrated states, which translates into "highest extinction of consciousness (perception)." As far as Poṭṭhapāda and his wanderers were concerned, it was the peak of spiritual experience, and they were anxious to learn more about it. Poṭṭhapāda continues:

> Some said: "One's perceptions arise and cease without cause or condition. When they arise, one is conscious, when they cease, then one is unconscious."

Poṭṭhapāda is saying that he has heard that the extinction of consciousness leads to unconsciousness. This is a crucial misunderstanding. Not unconsciousness, but a ceasing of perception and feeling is experienced. The Buddha will go on to explain this later in the sutta.

> That is how they explained it. But somebody else said: "No, that is not how it is. Perceptions are a person's self, which comes and goes. When it comes, one is conscious; when it goes, one is unconscious."

Poṭṭhapāda repeats someone else's opinion and is using the word for "highest perception of the extinction of consciousness," which in this context is entirely wrong, as the Buddha will tell him later.

> Another said: "That is not how it is. There are ascetics and Brahmins of great powers, of great influence. They draw down consciousness into a man and withdraw it. When they draw it down into him, he is conscious; when they withdraw it, he is unconscious." And another said: "No, that is not how it is. There are deities of great powers, of great influence. They draw down consciousness into a man and withdraw it. When they draw it down into him, he is conscious; when they withdraw it, he is unconscious."

There has always been a great deal of superstition in India, and these ideas sprang from it. The Buddha was adamant that superstition and outer events could never lead to a realization of the truth. Poṭṭhapāda went on:

> It was in this connection that I thought of the Lord: "Ah, sure-ly, the Blessed Lord, the Well-Farer, he is supremely skilled about these matters! The Blessed Lord well understands the higher extinction of consciousness." What then, Lord, is this higher extinction of consciousness?

Reading this sutta we get a feeling for the time in which the Buddha lived and his entire social surroundings. We become acquainted with the people he knew, almost as if we had been present. Eventually, they become our friends, and we are well aware of their habits and concerns. We recognize Poṭṭhapāda's deep respect for the Buddha in his question.

> In this matter, Poṭṭhapāda, those ascetics and Brahmins who say one's perceptions arise and cease without cause or condition are totally wrong.

The Buddha had no qualms about pronouncing some doctrines as erroneous. If they were wrong, he said so; when they were correct, he would affirm that they were right.

> "Why is that? One's perceptions arise and cease owing to a cause and conditions. Some perceptions arise through training, and some pass away through training. What is this training?" the Lord said.

The Buddha is not going to answer the original question yet, because the extinction of higher consciousness is very much the result of excellent training. Instead, he is going to start at the very beginning of this training.

> Poṭṭhapāda, a Tathāgata arises in this world, an Arahant...

Literally translated, *Tathāgata* means "one gone such." *Gata* is "gone," *tatha* is "such." It means "a Buddha."

...fully enlightened Buddha, endowed with wisdom and conduct, Well-Farer, Knower of the worlds, incomparable Trainer
of men to be tamed, Teacher of gods and humans, enlightened
and blessed.

These are traditional words describing the Buddha's qualities, which
are often chanted, and we can assume they are insertions into the text.

He, having realized it by his own super-knowledge, proclaims
this world with its devas, māras, and Brahmās...

*Devas* are what we call angels. In our culture we think of angels as eter-
nally angelic, but according to the Buddha, devas can fall from their high
state and be reborn as humans. Then they have to practice to regain the
deva world. At the start of each meditation course I always silently invite
them to join us. Those who wish to do that, appear. There is no gross body
in the deva realm, consequently very little dukkha, so that devas do not
have the same incentive to practice as we do. But some of them are happy
and willing to listen to the Dhamma and meditate with us.

Māras are devils. In this text the word is in the plural, but the exact
translation is "the tempter." In fact we all have both devas and māras within us, temptations and angelic purity. *Brahmās* are gods who occupy the
four highest realms of consciousness. There is no one creator, but there is
the realm of creation.

...its princes and people. He preaches the Dhamma which is
lovely in its beginning, lovely in its middle, lovely in its ending, in the spirit and in the letter...

A very important aspect of the Buddha's teaching is his emphasis on
meaning as well as words. It is relatively easy to know the texts; all we need
to do is read a book and try to remember as much of it as we can. Not
only scholars, but many other people as well, find this the most interesting part. But it is certainly not enough for a religious life. The spirit of the
message of our great religious leaders can only enter our hearts when we
practice. Then we come to know exactly what the Buddha meant, and his

guidelines become an integral part of our thoughts, speech, and action. Until then, all we have are words and intellectual understanding.

...and displays the fully-perfected and purified holy life.

The teaching of the Buddha is called the Dhamma. He did not teach Buddhism, any more than Jesus taught Christianity. The one wanted to reform Judaism, the other to reform Brahmanism. Neither succeeded, but each unwittingly started a new religion. The movements they started were reforms of ancient religions which, because the spirit had left them and only the letter still was observed, had deteriorated into rites and rituals, and social norms. Today we come across this very same problem everywhere.

A disciple goes forth and practices the moralities.

Going forth usually means becoming a monk or nun, but we can certainly practice morality as laypersons. Monks and nuns are, so to speak, compelled to adhere to their rules of conduct, and if they lack the spirit of the Dhamma within, they sometimes rebel. For a layperson, taking on the practice voluntarily, because of insight into its benefits, it may be even less of a struggle.

The Buddha has no intention of answering the question about higher states of consciousness yet. He first advocates practicing moral conduct as a foundation for spiritual development.

He now goes on to talk about the five moral precepts which constitute a basic attitude of restraint.

...he dwells refraining from taking life, without stick or sword, scrupulous, compassionate, trembling for the welfare of all living beings.

Here the Buddha emphasizes not only refraining from killing, but also practicing the opposite, namely, compassion and heartfelt concern for all beings.

The second precept is worded:

...[he] dwells refraining from taking of what is not given, living purely, accepting what is given, awaiting what is given, without stealing.

While the first precept counteracts our inner hate, the second one turns against greed. At other times, the Buddha recommends generosity as a countermeasure that helps us to let go of "me" and "mine" and think more in terms of helpfulness, togetherness, and love for others.

Abandoning unchastity, [he] lives far from it, aloof from the village-practice of sex.

The third precept, "to refrain from sexual misconduct," is changed here to "celibacy," because on the higher levels of the spiritual path, celibacy is considered a most important aspect of the training. For monks and nuns, it stands at the apex of their rules. If this precept is known to have been broken, the errant monk or nun is expelled from the Sangha, the ordained community. Laypersons sometimes go on three- or six-month retreats, during which time they observe the vow of celibacy. This fosters a sense of independence and helps to overcome strong sensual desire.

The fourth precept is given a long paragraph:

He dwells refraining from false speech, a truth-speaker, one to be relied on, trustworthy, dependable, not a deceiver of the world. Abandoning malicious speech, he does not repeat there what he has heard here to the detriment of these, or repeat here what he has heard there to the detriment of those. Thus he is a reconciler of those at variance and an encourager of those at one, rejoicing in peace, loving it, delighting in it, one who speaks up for peace. Abandoning harsh speech, he refrains from it. He speaks whatever is blameless, pleasing to the ear, agreeable, reaching the heart, urbane, pleasing and attractive to the multitude. Abandoning idle chatter, he speaks at the right time, what is correct and to the point, of Dhamma and discipline. He is a speaker whose words are to be treasured, seasonable, reasoned, well-defined and connected with the goal.

"A deceiver of the world" is a hypocrite, who says one thing and does another. Most of us have an inner register that can tell us whether the words we hear come from genuine experience or whether they are only empty shells—the letter without the spirit.

"Thus he is a reconciler of those at variance and an encourager of those at one, rejoicing in peace...." Here the important point is being made that peace can arise from speech. We have thousands of books that reach the mind but not the heart. When speech is strictly intellectual, it does not touch our feelings, but when the words we speak or write come from inner experience and are heartfelt, they are always imbued with "trembling for the welfare of beings."

"Abandoning idle chatter, he speaks at the right time, what is correct and to the point." In another discourse, the Buddha said that if we speak about the Dhamma, we should use precision of expression, what we say should be well thought out and easy to understand.

"A speaker whose words are...connected with the goal." The goal of the Buddha's teaching is *Nibbāna* (Sanskrit: *Nirvāṇa*). Literally translated, that means "not burning," or in other words, the loss of all passions. Often on hearing this for the first time, we might feel that we don't really want to lose all our passionate reactions. That is perfectly all right, but in that case our purpose and goal are of a different nature. However, most of us can agree with the Buddha when he says that speech should be edifying, inspiring, reaching the heart, and that Dhamma language should be correct and to the point. Such speech is directed toward the loss of dukkha, and that is a well-understood and universal goal. The question is, How can it be done? We need to find a connection between "I don't want to let go of my passions" and "I would like to lose all my dukkha," by investigating our reactions, to find how our dukkha arises. This can be used as a contemplative enquiry: "When do I have dukkha?" "Where does it come from?" "Why do I get it?" Every answer will serve as a new question. Should we be convinced that we have no dukkha, then we might ask ourselves, why do we want to meditate? This is an important contemplation, because it will facilitate the step between our wish for no more dukkha and our ability to find its causes and rid ourselves of them once and for all.

The fifth precept, to avoid alcohol and drugs, does not appear here. Instead we are told the disciple "refrains from damaging seeds and crops."

In some Buddhist countries, due to social conditioning, this is often mis-interpreted as meaning that a monk or nun cannot work in the garden. We can see, however, that it concerns damage and does not refer at all to the care and growth of plants. Because in this sutta the Buddha is teaching ascetics, who are already on the spiritual path and want to know about the highest aspects of it, he is probably taking it for granted that alcohol and drugs are not part of their lives and therefore omits that precept. The Buddha continues with those precepts taken by novice monks or nuns, or laypersons for a limited period of intensive practice. They include: "refraining from eating at improper times." For us today, that could mean not going to the refrigerator and helping ourselves to something out of it any time we feel like it, or not keeping a bar of chocolate in our pocket and nibbling at it whenever we please. It denotes using a certain amount of discipline in our eating habits. Should we want to practice a stricter self-discipline, then we might eat only one meal a day, or at certain times, we might choose to fast.

"He avoids watching dancing, singing, music and shows." All these are distractions and geared to arousing sexual desire. They are connected to greed, or the wish for sensual gratification. If we want to practice very intensely, we are better off not attending such entertainment, so that the mind may stay in an even-minded repose.

"He abstains from using garlands, perfumes, cosmetics, ornaments and adornments." It is common practice in the world to expend much effort on making ourselves look more attractive. This is simply a support system for our attachment to the self-illusion. If we are rich, we can adorn ourselves with valuable things; that supports our sense of self-worth. "If I have valuable things, I must be a valuable person." The thought may not be clearly articulated, but that is what lies at the bottom of it.

"He avoids accepting gold and silver." This means not going into business, but also refers to being frugal, living simply and not hankering after worldly profits. Then follows a list of things that were given as *dāna,* or offerings, to the monks in those days and which should not be accepted: "raw grain or raw flesh, he does not accept women and young girls, male or female slaves, sheep and goats, cocks and pigs, elephants, cattle, horses and mares, fields and plots...." These gifts are temptations to live a more mundane life and to relegate the spiritual path to the background.

...he refrains from running errands, from buying and selling, from cheating with false weights and measures, from bribery and corruption, deception and insincerity, from wounding, killing, imprisoning, highway robbery, and taking food by force.

It is interesting to note that when the Buddha first ordained monks and nuns, none of these precepts were articulated. He simply said the words: *Ehi bhikkhu,* "Come, monk" and that was sufficient to follow the Buddha into the homeless life. But since monks and nuns are as fallible as anyone and give way to worldly temptations, the Buddha eventually formulated rules of conduct, which are still valid to this day.

Deception and insincerity are defilements that easily enter into the hearts of unenlightened people. We may not feel very much identified with some of the other admonitions, yet we can utilize the Buddha's instructions on restraint by letting go of habits that are prevalent in the marketplace and are detrimental to more intensive practice. We shall eventually find out the answer to Poṭṭhapāda's original question, but the Buddha's teaching expositions would usually begin with everyday life, then proceed, step by step to meditation, and finally to insight into the nature of absolute reality.

# 2

# Guarding the Senses:
# Mindfulness and Clear Comprehension

Having explained this first step to Poṭṭhapāda, the Buddha now tells him:

> …that monk who is perfected in morality sees no danger from any side owing to his being restrained by morality.

To perfect anything takes training. It is wise, however, not to think of this training as something imposed on us from outside. Rather, it is something we impose on ourselves because we realize that by conquering our own negative instincts and impulses, we will eventually conquer all the illusions that create dukkha for us. Every step of the Buddha's teaching is designed to take us nearer to that goal. "Seeing no danger from any side" obviously brings a feeling of security. Knowing we have done nothing wrong, we have no guilt, no sense of omission or commission, and therefore we feel very much at ease.

The Buddha gives a simile:

> Just as a duly-anointed Khattiya king, having conquered his enemies, by that very fact sees no danger from any side, so the monk, on account of his morality, sees no danger anywhere. He experiences in himself the blameless bliss that comes from maintaining this Ariyan morality.

The word "bliss" denotes an inner joy. It is not meditative bliss, which we will discuss in a later chapter, but a feeling of contentment that comes from knowing ourselves to be blameless and in no danger from our passions. *Ariyan* means "noble," and Ariyan morality demands a greater degree of renunciation than simply keeping the five precepts; as we saw, for instance, the third precept—to refrain from sexual misconduct—changes here to abstention, or celibacy.

The Buddha now moves on to the next step, "guarding the sense-doors." He still makes no attempt to answer Poṭṭhapāda's question about the higher extinction of consciousness. It is clear he knows at this stage that Poṭṭhapāda would be incapable of understanding the answer.

> Here a monk, on seeing a visible object with the eye, does not grasp at its major signs or secondary characteristics. Because greed and sorrow, evil unskilled states, would overwhelm him if he dwelt leaving this eye-faculty unguarded, so he practices guarding it, he protects the eye-faculty, develops restraint of the eye-faculty.

This is then repeated for the other senses:

> On hearing a sound with the ear,…on smelling an odour with the nose,…on tasting a flavour with the tongue,…on feeling an object with the body,…on thinking a thought with the mind…

Then, the Buddha says:

> He experiences within himself the blameless bliss that comes from maintaining this Ariyan guarding of the faculties. In this way…a monk is a guardian of the sense-doors.

Most of the time, this is misunderstood and wrongly practiced. It is taken to mean, not to look, not to hear, not to taste, not to touch. This is quite impossible. Our senses are there; we must look, hear, taste, touch, smell. Our mind refuses not to think, as we very well know from our meditation. Yet this kind of practice is frequently taught.

Of course it is true that if we do not look at something, we will not be perturbed by it. But how can we avoid looking, particularly in ordinary, everyday life? It is extremely important to understand what is being said in this passage, particularly if we would like to live according to the moral precepts. "(He) does not grasp at its major signs or secondary characteristics." When the eye sees, it simply registers color and shape. All the rest takes place in the mind. For instance, we see a piece of chocolate. The eye sees only the brown shape. It is the mind that says: "Ah, chocolate! That tastes delicious—I want a piece!" Not to grasp at the major signs or secondary characteristics is to stop the mind from doing exactly that.

We can practice this quite easily with anything we either very much like or very much dislike. The two strongest senses are seeing and hearing, so we should pick one of those and watch how the mind reacts, become aware of the inner story telling. It is not possible for the ear or the eye to decide what is seen or heard. For example, the ear hears the sound of a truck. The mind says "truck." Then it says, "Very noisy. Most unpleasant. No wonder I can't meditate." All that comes from the mind; it has nothing to do with the sound itself. Sound is just sound, color is just color, shape is just shape.

People who undertake the precept of celibacy are sometimes advised not to look at members of the opposite sex. But how can anyone do that? I have met monks who have attempted it, but it leads to stilted, awkward relationships. How can you talk to someone who is deliberately not looking at you? This is not what is meant by guarding the sense-doors. Rather, when the eye has seen the shape, and the mind has said "man," or "woman," we stop there. We do not allow the mind to add more. Whatever else it may say will give rise to greed or hate, depending on the situation. Most of us are capable of practicing this, and in fact if we do, it can make life much easier. Let us suppose that, we go shopping. We take with us our sensible list of all the things we really need. Then our eye falls on the huge array of other goods for sale, all beautifully packaged, all available to us, some perhaps on special offer. Immediately, the mind becomes interested, and we end up buying far more than we needed. Some of us actually go shopping in order to find things that attract us, and buy them as a kind of hobby, as a weekend outing, if we have the money.

If we are easily swayed by what we see, the best thing to do is to recognize the sense-contact and stop the mind at the perception, the labeling. It is very hard to stop it before that. So, for example, if we see a person, or even think of a person, for whom we have hate or greed, someone we either dislike or long for intensely, we should practice stopping at the label, person, friend, male, female. Nothing further. The rest is our desire. That is what is meant by guarding the sense-doors.

Our senses are our survival system. It is much easier to survive if we can see and hear than if we are blind or deaf. Most people assume, however, that the senses are there in order to provide them with pleasure. We use them in that way and become angry when they fail to do so. We then blame the trigger. If someone displeases us, we blame that person. It has nothing to do with the other person, who, like us, is made up of the four elements, has the same senses, the same limbs, and is looking, as we are, for happiness. There is nothing in that person that is producing displeasure. It is all in our own mind.

Exactly the same applies when we think another person will provide us with pleasure. Here again we have someone made up of the four elements, with the same senses, the same limbs, the same wish for happiness as ourselves. There is no reason to look to that person for pleasure or blame them for not providing it. All we have to do is see "person." Nothing more. There are so many "persons" in this world, why should we allow this particular one to arouse our syndrome of desire-distaste?

If we guard our senses, we guard our passions, which enables us to live with far greater equanimity. We are no longer on that endless seesaw; up, when we are getting what we want, down, when we are not, which induces a continual inner feeling of wanting something that just escapes us. Nothing that is to be had in the world, anywhere, under any circumstances, is capable of bringing fulfillment. All that the world can provide are sense-contacts—seeing, hearing, tasting, touching, smelling, and thinking. All are short-lived and have to be renewed, over and over again. This takes time and energy, and here again it is not the sense-contact itself that satisfies us. It is what the mind makes of it. Guarding the sense-doors is one of the most important things we can do, if we want to lead a peaceful, harmonious life, untroubled by wanting what we do not have, or not wanting what we do have. These are the only two causes for dukkha; there are no others. If we watch our sense-contacts and do not go past the labeling, we have a very good chance of being at ease.

The mind is a magician—it can produce a magic show any time. The minute we go past the perception (labeling) that is what it will do, and we shall find ourselves drawn to either hate or greed. The Buddha mentions Māra, the tempter. Māra is constantly with us, waiting for an opening. Temptations are unnecessary. Where they exist, we need to overcome them, but we do not even need to have them in the first place. We can stop before they start, and that means guarding the senses.

The Buddha still has much to say to Poṭṭhapāda about what he needs to practice, before giving him any teaching on meditation and the higher extinction of consciousness. He comes now to the subject of mindfulness and clear comprehension. This is the way his teaching progresses in many of his discourses: first, morality; then guarding the sense-doors; then mindfulness and clear comprehension. The last two are companions, often mentioned together. *Sati* is mindfulness, and *sampajañña* is clear comprehension. In this translation, "comprehension" is translated as "awareness."

> And how...is a monk accomplished in mindfulness and clear awareness? Here a monk acts with clear awareness in going forth and back, in looking ahead or behind him, in bending and stretching, in wearing his outer and inner robe and carrying his bowl, in eating, drinking, chewing and swallowing, in evacuating and urinating, in walking, standing, sitting, lying down, in waking, in speaking and in keeping silent he acts with clear awareness. In this way, a monk is accomplished in mindfulness and clear awareness.

Mindfulness has four aspects: body, emotions, underlying mood, and content of thought. Mindfulness of the body, to which the Buddha is referring in this passage, takes pride of place. It is essential to practice mindfulness in our everyday life, not simply during our meditation periods. If there is no mindfulness outside of meditation, there will be none within it. The two go hand in hand. So we practice this first foundation of mindfulness by watching our body. We become aware of what we are doing, whether we are walking, standing, sitting, lying down, getting dressed or undressed, stretching, bending—whatever it may be. One of the advantages of being mindful of the body is that while we practice, we are also keeping the mind in its place, not allowing it to roam discursively.

A second advantage is that mindfulness purifies. If we are actually watching what we are doing, we cannot in that moment be upset, angry, or greedy. The Buddha counsels us over and over to use the body as a mindfulness-object. In the first place, we can feel the body and touch it; we do not have to search for its presence. If we practice in this way, we will realize in a very short time the peacefulness that arises, the absence of all mental turmoil. For how can we be aggravated, or desirous, or disliking while we are watching what is actually happening?

Thirdly, body-mindfulness keeps us in the present moment, and eventually we may learn that there is no other moment. To be in the present is actually to be in eternity. Usually, we establish boundaries between moments: the past moment, the present one, and the one to come. We see them as three, but in fact we can only be in one, the present. The other two are mind-made; they are fantasies created from memories or imagination. Most people live in the past, the future, or in a blend of the two, and if we do that, then mindfulness and meditation will be extremely difficult for us, for they are both happening now.

To be aware of our emotions and what we are feeling is the second foundation of mindfulness. The fourth (we'll get to the third in a moment) is content of thought, and both it and the second are addressed in meditation and need to be continued in daily life. For instance, should a strong emotion arise, we first recognize its content and then try to substitute the wholesome for the unwholesome. We do not have to believe every one of our emotions. If we go back to their source, we will invariably find they are due to a sense-contact. It is most illuminating to check this out. The same applies to the contents of our thoughts. If we recognize them as wholesome, we simply note that, and as they subside, we return to mindfulness of the body. Should they be unwholesome, we substitute as quickly as we can. The less time we allow the unwholesome to stay with us, the less chance there is of developing deep ruts of negativity in the mind. The more we become aware of our greed, which is an overall word for "wanting," and our hate, which is an overall word for "not wanting," and the less time we give either of them to settle into the mind, the easier it becomes to free ourselves from them.

The third foundation of mindfulness is our underlying mood. This too is an important object of attention. If we can catch the unwholesome mood before it develops into thinking or emotion, then substitution becomes a much easier task. Some people have an underlying mood that is constantly negative and find it very hard to change. Most of us alternate between positive and negative. There are also those whose mood is mainly positive. If we find it to be one of resentment, envy, or dislike resulting in negative thinking and negative emotions, then we can try to tackle the mood itself, recognizing as we do so that it is nothing but a mood and has no deeper significance. Nothing that we have, or think, or do has any basic and profound importance. It is simply happening. We do not have to retain the thought content, the emotion, or the mood, if they are detrimental to our own happiness. The more happiness we ourselves experience, the more we can give to others. It is quite impossible to give what we ourselves do not have. Why people should believe themselves capable of that is a mystery.

These are the four foundations of mindfulness: body, emotion, mood, and content of thought. Mindfulness means paying bare attention; there is nothing judgmental about it. It is clear comprehension that knows whether the sensation, emotion, mood, or thought-process is wholesome or unwholesome, and enables us to substitute. Each of us is capable of clearly comprehending; we have sufficient wisdom to do that. We also have, of course, all the human foibles, those constant creators of unhappiness, worry, restlessness, and agitation, but we do not need to hold on to them. With clear comprehension we can recognize this and begin to substitute the wholesome for the unwholesome. We practice this in meditation, learning to let each discursive thought go and putting our attention back on the meditation subject, and in just the same way we practice in everyday life.

The only reason people retain their negativities is because they justify them, putting the blame on someone or something in the world outside of themselves. This does not bring happiness. On the inner journey we have the opportunity to see ourselves as we really are and not as we would like to appear in society or to others.

Seeing ourselves plainly, we can change, and as we do so, it brings a feeling of great relief, as if we had dropped a heavy load. Simply to be mindful relieves us of the burden of discursive thinking and reacting. Constantly reacting to the world around us takes mental energy and is often critical and judgmental. With mindfulness none of that happens.

Mindfulness means we watch our step, literally and figuratively, under all circumstances. Of course we will forget, there is no doubt about that, but the minute we remember again, we are back on track. It is the most helpful thing we can do for ourselves.

Clear comprehension has four aspects, not mentioned in this particular text. The first is to become aware of what we are intending to say or do, and to investigate whether its purpose is beneficial or not. If it is self-centered and self-cherishing, it is unlikely to be so. Once we have decided that it is beneficial, the second aspect is to ascertain whether we actually have the skillful means on hand for what we have decided to do or say. Could they be more skillful? The third aspect is to ask ourselves what the purpose and the means are within the Dhamma. Another way of putting this would be to ask: Would the Buddha approve? We check our purpose and we check our means against what we know of the teaching. Primarily, we check to see whether it is compatible with the precepts, whether it is within the context of loving-kindness and compassion and conducive to happiness. Is it directed toward the goal of eventually losing all dukkha? This is an important question because otherwise we are likely to get sidetracked. The world offers such multiple possibilities that unless we reflect first, we will find it almost impossible to refrain from the unwholesome. If our answer to these questions has been affirmative, then we go ahead with our action. As a fourth step, having done or said what we intended to do or say, we investigate whether we have actually accomplished our purpose, and if not, why not? Where was it lacking?

This is one way of explaining clear comprehension, the one that will be the most useful to us in everyday life. First we need mindfulness in order to become aware of what is going on within us. Then we check out our intentions in the light of clear comprehension. Practicing in this way slows down our reactions, and that is all to the good. When we act impulsively, it is only too easy to make mistakes, but when we deliberate a little more, we are far more likely to move in a positive direction.

Next, the Buddha talks of contentment with our daily needs:

> And how is a monk contented? Here, a monk is satisfied with a robe to protect his body, with alms to satisfy his stomach, and having accepted a sufficient amount, he goes on his way. Just as a bird with wings flies hither and thither, burdened by nothing but its wings, so he is satisfied.

In the industrialized societies of today, most people have more than they need. The Buddha said four things are necessary: food, shelter, clothing, and medicine to cure the body when it falls ill. Those are our material needs. Obviously, most of us have at least ten dozen other things that we think we cannot do without, and though some of them may indeed be necessary, the rest probably are not. It is well worth our while to check out need against greed, and see where that takes us. Having done that, we then ask ourselves: "Am I contented with my material situation? Am I grateful for it? Do I realize that having enough is a great blessing, one that is denied to many people on this globe?" Do we in fact remember those others who do not have enough to eat, nor enough clothing, nor any medicine, nor a roof over their heads? Are we taking it for granted, we who have all that? Usually, we are. In fact we complain when what we have does not look quite as we would like it to look, or taste the way we would like it to taste, or is different from what we are accustomed to, and we don't want the change. We find it easier to complain, than to be grateful for everything we have.

The Buddha was once walking along the seashore with his monks and said to them: "Monks, imagine that there is a blind turtle swimming in the oceans of the world, and that turtle comes up for air only once in a hundred years. There is also a wooden yoke floating in the oceans of the world. Do you think, monks, that when that turtle comes up for air, it could put its head through that wooden yoke?" The monks said, "No, sir, that is impossible." The Buddha answered, "It is not impossible. It is improbable." He went on to say that the same improbability reigns over the chances of being born a human being, with all senses and limbs intact and with the opportunity of hearing the true.

Do we ourselves remember to think along those lines in order to cultivate contentment? In meditation, contentment is a vital ingredient. The less content the mind, the less it will be able to meditate, for to be discontented is to be in a state of agitation. We become discontented because we think our meditation is not working properly, or we want it to produce something more significant, or we want to become enlightened, or whatever else we may be wanting, which it is not providing. This agitation and discontent only make matters worse. It is useless to meditate unless we first arouse contentment. Otherwise our meditation simply deteriorates, while our discontent grows bigger and bigger. Anything we practice, we become better at, so if we practice discontent, we become highly proficient at being discontented. It becomes an inner reality: "I am not content because…" and then we give any number of reasons for our dissatisfaction, most of them quite foolish and none of them having to do with our basic needs for clothing, food, shelter, or medicine.

We should remember what the Buddha said about the chances of being born as a human being and having the opportunity to hear the Dhamma and remember too that we have everything we need to sustain life so that we may continue to practice. When we have a mind that is full of gratitude for our excellent situation, for the great opportunity we have been given, then and only then will we be able to meditate. The discontented mind rushes from one place to the next trying to find something that will bring it contentment. Meditation can certainly provide that, but in order for it to do so, we must first cultivate an inner attitude of contentment and gratitude for what we have.

The four basic needs are known as the Four Requisites. In our day and age, of course, there are many other things we may need, possibly in order to make a living, or to communicate, but they are in a sense extraneous. We could sustain life without them. It is very helpful to take the time to contemplate all the things for which we can be grateful and put everything else out of our mind. In everyone's life there will inevitably be some things that are not satisfactory, that arouse discontent. If we contemplate these, they will grow out of proportion and fill our thoughts. If, on the other hand, we put our mind on all there is in our lives that is truly good, truly satisfying, then it will be our contentment that grows and expands. It is really quite simple. Whatever we put our mind on, that is what we know. We are not obliged to think negative thoughts, yet we constantly do. It is another of our human foibles. We put our minds on such matters, which are bound to make us unhappy. Even though we know already that doing this will make us suffer, we still do it. Perhaps we should contemplate why we think in ways that we know perfectly well will create unhappiness? The more clearly we see into our inner processes, the easier it will be to discard those that are not helpful, that do not lead to calm and contentment.

Contentment with our life as it is brings a feeling of great lightness, for we lose the burden of continually craving for situations and people to be different. Things are as they are. Refusing to accept this creates dukkha and brings pain. It is like pushing against a sealed door. We push and we push until our hands hurt, but we cannot open it. If we are wise, we accept that this is simply how it is. The door is sealed, and it is perfectly all right that it is so.

It is the same with our lives. Things are the way they are and this is all right; it is the way they are supposed to be. There are causes and effects, though we will usually not be able to see them clearly. That does not matter. What matters is to see that our lives, moment by moment, are providing us with a learning situation. When something comes up that we do not like, that we find unsatisfactory, the very first thing to do is to ask ourselves what we can learn from it. Rather than pushing against it and wishing it were different, which is guaranteed to produce dukkha, we enquire: "Am I learning anything from this?" Not to learn from our experiences is a tremendous waste of time.

Life is an adult-education school. If we look at it in this light, we see it correctly. If we expect it to be geared to pleasure, we are bound to be disappointed. For many of us this is exactly what happens, until it eventually dawns on us that we are here to learn.

In this adult-education school, all topics are addressed. Each of us is given the one that is appropriate to his or her class, which has nothing to do with age but is more concerned with inner development. We are confronted with what we need to learn. If we do not learn it, do not pass the examination, we will find ourselves back in the same class again, being presented with exactly the same lesson. Only when we pass the examination appropriate for our inner being, can we move on to the next class, the next topic.

Poṭṭhapāda, too, must learn each lesson. Morality, guarding the senses, mindfulness, clear comprehension, all lead toward the higher extinction of consciousness. But Poṭṭhapāda must understand and practice each of them on his journey toward that final goal.

## 3

# Setting Aside the Hindrances

Then he, equipped with this Ariyan morality, with this Ariyan restraint of the senses, with this Ariyan contentment, finds a solitary lodging, at the root of a forest tree, in a mountain cave or gorge, a charnel-ground, a jungle-thicket, or in the open air on a heap of straw. Then, having eaten after his return from the alms-round, he sits down cross-legged, holding his body erect, and concentrates on keeping mindfulness established before him.

In this passage, the Buddha broaches the subject of meditation itself. However, as we shall see in a moment, there is more to do than simply sit cross-legged, "keeping mindfulness established." Before *ānāpānasati*, mindfulness of in-breath and out-breath, can really result in any significant change of consciousness—which meditation is designed to bring about—it is necessary to free ourselves from five hindrances, which the Buddha now lists:

1. Worldly Desire

Abandoning worldly desires, he dwells with a mind freed from worldly desires, and his mind is purified of them.

This hindrance is very often called "the desire for sensual gratification." It is obvious we will not be able to meditate if we are burdened by any such longings. We need to make an inner determination to let them go. Desires that often beset a meditator are: "It's too cold, it's too hot, my knees hurt, my back is uncomfortable, I'm hungry, I've eaten too much, I want something to drink, I don't feel well, I need to sleep." Any such thought, when it enters the mind, will bring our meditation to a halt.

Everything that comes to us through our senses comes from the world, but the inner experience that comes to us through meditation is not dependent on worldly matters. Once we are able to experience the joy of full concentration, we will find that this in itself is an automatic antidote to desire. If the mind is one-pointed, no worldly desire can enter. The more often we are able to achieve this one-pointedness, the less we will have to struggle against our longing for food, comfort, warmth, or whatever else it may be we want or do not want. All dukkha comes from desire, and the more we want something, the more dukkha we have. Even to think "I want a good meditation" is a worldly desire.

Our desires are related to the belief that happiness comes through our sense-contacts. We all, of course, have happy moments, and that is as it should be; but when we continually search for those particular sense-contacts that we imagine will bring us gratification, we block our path to meditation, to purification, and to the way out of dukkha. As long as we are immersed in desire, we are immersed in suffering. This is totally unnecessary. All we have to do is let the desire go. It is easily said, but not, of course, so simple to do. It is a matter of understanding and will power.

The monkey trap will illustrate this. In India hunters fashion a monkey trap out of twigs and branches. It is funnel shaped with a narrow open end and a larger closed base. A sweet is placed in the closed base, and for the monkey to reach the sweet, he has to put his paw into the narrow funnel. But when he has closed his fist around the sweet, he can't pull his paw out of the narrow funnel any more. He is trapped and prey to the hunter. All he would have to do to be free would be to let go of the sweet he craves. If he were to open his fist, he could easily escape. Exactly the same is true for us, but we also find it most difficult to let go of what we desire.

Once we have seen how our dukkha arises and that meditation can only go well when we are free of all these thoughts concerning worldly likes and dislikes, we may then recognize that by dropping the desire we can make the thoughts cease. Once we start to practice this, we immediately begin to see the results. We must be careful not to fall into the trap of a tight, intense wishing for results. That in itself is dukkha and arises from worldly desire: "I want this; I want it badly." Any such longing should be dropped. There is nothing to be desired; there is everything to be done. We recognize what is necessary, what the task in hand is, and we simply carry it out.

The Buddha gave similes for each hindrance. Sensual desire is likened to being in debt. We are in debt to our sense-contacts, which have to be constantly renewed, constantly repaid. Unless we know better, gratification of our sense-contacts will be all we are concerned with, and when we do not get what we hope for, or it does not last, we will become very unhappy and angry at something or someone. This is quite unrealistic because nothing that comes to us through the senses can be retained, be it a sight, sound, smell, taste, touch, or a thought. It all comes and goes, and is dependent on outer conditions over which we have very little jurisdiction, if indeed any at all.

Being in debt, always needing to repay our loan, means that we are continually worried about or looking for those pleasant sense-contacts. When the realization comes to us that this search is really quite unnecessary, it is as if we had paid off the loan. There is no longer any debt to the senses which, as the Buddha said, is something to rejoice and be glad about. Knowing we do not have to follow our sensual desires brings a great feeling of security and independence, whereas when we follow our sensual desires, we are in a constant state of agitation.

## 2. Ill-Will

> Abandoning ill-will and hatred…and by compassionate love for the welfare of all living beings, his mind is purified of ill-will and hatred.

Ill-will is entirely counterproductive, both in our everyday lives and when we sit down to meditate. This is why we should begin every meditation with thoughts of compassionate love for the welfare of all living beings, starting with ourselves. Some of us find it very difficult to love ourselves. We are full of self-criticism and self-dislike. If this is the case, then it will be even harder for us to let go of our desires, for somehow we believe that gratifying desires will make us feel good about ourselves and thus produce the missing link, namely, self-acceptance and self-compassion. But no gratified desire will ever do that. It simply produces more dukkha, because it is recurrent, demanding to be satisfied over and over again. The missing link can only come through the practice of loving-kindness toward ourselves, in spite of everything we know about ourselves. Only then, in fact, will we be able to love others, without criticism or judgment.

Perfectionism has no place in compassionate love. On a worldly level, nothing is perfect; it never has been and never will be. The unnecessary concept that things and people ought to be perfect creates tension and constriction because it arouses a want. By dropping this false ideal, and thereby letting go of the desire, we will experience much relaxation and relief.

Should we find it hard to feel loving-kindness for ourselves, there are two ways of arousing it that can be particularly helpful. The first is to think of the person we love most and transfer that feeling to ourselves. It must not be connected with desire, for then it will not be effective. It must be a pure feeling of caring, embracing, wanting to help, a feeling of connectedness. A second way is to remember all the good things we have done in this life. Remembrance brings them into the present, and experiencing them in the present allows us to feel at ease with ourselves. We are able, at this moment, to love the person who acted with goodness of heart.

When we have directed this feeling of loving-kindness toward ourselves, we should then think of the multitude of beings existing on this planet, all of them searching for peace and happiness and very few finding it, and extend our compassionate love to them also.

If we harbor bad feelings toward others—perhaps those who are close to us or with whom we come into daily contact—we should remember that the more we abandon ill-will and hatred, the easier it will be to meditate. The Buddha said that a mind that is full of ill-will and aware of it at the time cannot possibly meditate. A mind imbued with love and compassion can do so, because love and compassion are a giving of ourselves. In meditation, we have to give ourselves totally, with no holding back. Whatever meditation subject we have chosen, we must become immersed in it; there can be no part of us left out, no "me" who wants to solve a particular problem or to work out how "I" can somehow still gratify my desires, even though I see the truth in what the Buddha said.

There is a discourse in which the Buddha talks about royal elephants who go into battle for their king. If an elephant goes to war and only uses his feet, he is not royal. If he only uses his head, keeping his body protected, he is not royal. If he only uses his trunk and protects the rest of his body, he is not royal. Only when he goes forward into war with his whole body, immersed in the service to his king, can he be called a royal elephant. This is very often the obstacle in meditation. We withhold parts of ourselves. We think: "What am I getting out of this? Is this really the right teaching? How am I to make my meditation go the way I want it? If I could fulfill this or that desire, wouldn't I lose my dukkha?" All these thoughts keep some part of us completely separate from the meditation. When the mind is unified and one-pointed, so that worldly desires cannot arise, it is also unified in the sense of entering completely into the meditation subject. It is no longer an observer but becomes the experiencer and, finally, becomes one with the experience. When that happens, we have full concentration.

Illness is the simile given by the Buddha for ill-will and hatred. We all know how it feels to be angry—hot, overwhelmed, and agitated—most unpleasant, to say the least. This is why it is sometimes said that those who have the most ill-will are the best practitioners, feeling so uncomfortable all the time gives them a great incentive to practice. The Buddha also compared hatred to a bilious disease, where bile keeps arising in the mind.

Ill-will or hatred is one of our unwholesome roots, of which there are three—hate, greed, and delusion. We also have three wholesome roots—love, generosity, and wisdom. It is entirely up to us which roots we choose to strengthen. Delusion means the false concept that there is an individual entity called "me," which must be protected, supported, looked after, and whose needs and demands must be constantly satisfied. Because of this delusion, we experience greed when we think we want something and hatred when we don't get it. We cannot attack delusion directly because hate and greed are too overpowering and block our view. We must first begin by working on these two available enemies, attempting to weaken their roots.

In our meditation time, for example, we let go of ill-will. Should there be anyone or anything we particularly dislike, we can start our meditation by saying to ourselves: "I shall let go of all dislike for this period of time." There is nothing to stop us picking it up again afterward, if that is what we want. If we are unable to let go of our anger at least temporarily, our meditation will not work. Letting go of hate and ill-will is like recovering from an illness.

### 3. Sloth and Torpor

> Abandoning sloth-and-torpor,…perceiving light, mindful and
> clearly aware, his mind is purified of sloth-and-torpor.

Laziness and drowsiness, which can beset us in meditation, are examples of sloth and torpor. The remedy given here is to "perceive light." There are two ways of doing this. Should the mind be really drowsy, on the verge of falling asleep, the best thing to do is to open the eyes and look directly into the light. When we regain the feeling of wakefulness, we close our eyes again and try to take that light into ourselves, keeping its brightness within us. Our drowsiness and laziness of mind, caused by lack of motivation and lack of right effort, are usually dissipated by that interior light. Right effort must not be tension and tightness in mind and body, but rather wakefulness and awareness.

When the meditating mind becomes drowsy, it no longer knows exactly what is going on. It is as if the ground on which it stands is waxed, so that it slithers around in all directions. It does not move into definite thoughts, nor does it have any real hold on the meditation subject. This is sloth and torpor. At this point, we should stop. It is tempting to try to continue with the meditation because the feeling in the mind is quite pleasant. We are hardly aware of the dukkha because the mind has reverted to a state where it is neither asleep nor awake. It is in a kind of limbo. It is important to get ourselves out of this situation immediately, for it is a complete waste of time. We should open our eyes, move the body to encourage blood circulation, pull our earlobes, and rub our cheeks. As a last resort, we should stand up. It helps to give ourselves a pep talk: "The time for meditation is now; let me make the best of it." Not with the aim of "getting something from it," but in the sense of doing our very best.

The perception of light within, when it comes spontaneously, is usually a sign that concentration has started. We can, however, arouse it deliberately and should do so whenever we feel that the mind is not quite attentive. Perhaps it has lost momentum or never really had any; perhaps we cannot even remember why we are meditating. If we put light in the mind, it illuminates those dark corners, where all the hindrances to our meditation are lurking.

The simile for sloth and torpor is that it is like being in prison. As drowsiness permeates us, we become incapable of action. Although we possess the key to the prison door, we are unable to use it. We need to arouse the necessary joy and effort by remembering or projecting a feeling of being uplifted. When joy and effort are both present, the mind feels inspired, and with an inspired mind we can meditate. The Buddha also said that knowing more of the Dhamma would be helpful.

4. Restlessness and Worry

> Abandoning worry-and-flurry... and with an inwardly calmed
> mind his heart is purified of worry-and-flurry.

"...[W]ith an inwardly calmed mind." We need to really look at what that means. We would like the meditation to bring us calm, but the Buddha is saying that we have to be calm in order to meditate. So what we have here is an injunction to recognize when there is agitation in the mind. We then need to find the reason for it. "Why am I not calm? What desire is disturbing me? Why am I restless?" When the mind cannot stay in one place, the body often follows suit. Restlessness arises from the fact that we are not getting what we want. So we should examine this agitation, pinpoint the desire, and ask ourselves whether gratifying it would really bring us the calm we need? Or can we simply drop it, thereby losing the dukkha that always accompanies desire, and the restlessness it brings in its wake, and thus calm the mind?

In this passage, the Buddha also says that "with an inwardly calmed mind his heart is purified...." It is not only that the mind is no longer agitated, but the absence of desire purifies the emotions too. The heart is at ease; there is a feeling of even-mindedness, of being connected to all that surrounds us, of not being worried by things that are missing. In reality, nothing is missing. We already have everything we need; our ideas and concepts prevent us from seeing this. If we were to drop those ideas, meditation would become much easier. One such idea is that we can become calm through some outer source. On the contrary, calm is within us and we get to it by letting go of all outer circumstances, which are only present through our thoughts. Restlessness and worry are always connected to desire, and when we recognize this and let go of the desire, the heart is purified and the mind is calmed.

Worry is very often concerned with the future and our wish that it should be the way we have planned. It is obviously an absurd way to live, for by focusing so closely on what may lie ahead of us, we make the present disappear. Yet the present moment is the only one we have, the only one that counts. Restlessness, as we have seen, is connected to our search for satisfaction in the outside world. When we realize that all we want already exists within us, we may find it easier to drop our constant unrest.

Many of us think we have far too much to do. It is very interesting to discover we have in fact brought all this activity on ourselves. What we do is what we have chosen to do, even though we complain about it later. Activity gives us a sense of importance and makes us feel we are "somebody." Restlessness causes a lot of difficulty in our everyday life, for it leads us into many different situations with which we are then obliged to deal, and finally we feel overwhelmed. We should see it for the hindrance it is.

The Buddha likened restlessness and worry to a state of slavery. We are pushed around by these emotions and allow them to be our masters. Worry fills our minds, so that we are no longer able to think independently. A meditator, however, has to become an independent thinker. This does not mean trying to invent a spiritual teaching and working everything out for ourselves. There is no need for that. The Buddha's guidelines are there for us to follow, and we are very lucky to have them. An independent mind, however, is able to make the connections between the different parts of the teaching, and understand for itself how they fit together. At first it seems like a jigsaw puzzle, made up of separate pieces, but gradually we begin to understand their interdependence and to see the beauty of the picture as a whole.

5. Skeptical Doubt

Abandoning doubt, he dwells with doubt left behind, without uncertainty as to what things are wholesome, his mind is purified of doubt.

In order to combat doubt, we need to know what is wholesome. We also need to know with what we should concern ourselves, what is conducive to the final goal of enlightenment. But at this point in the sutta the goal is calmness of mind, which we need in order to meditate. Doubt prevents us from experiencing tranquility. Perhaps we doubt we are capable of meditating and fear it is too difficult for us. Perhaps we doubt the instructions and wonder whether we really need to follow them. Long years of experience have shown that those who follow the instructions have excellent results. These instructions derive from a tradition two thousand five hundred years old and are totally trustworthy, totally reliable. They have worked over and over again. Our own ideas, however, are based on viewpoints. Personal views are connected with self-image and our place in the world; they are neither reliable nor trustworthy. It is very important to internalize the Buddha's instructions and follow them wholeheartedly, so that there is no room in our minds for doubt. We are very fond of using our minds to conjure up all sorts of ideas and possibilities, which might prove the Buddha wrong. This is a favorite pastime, particularly when our meditation is not going well. "There must be something wrong with the teaching. I'm trying hard, so it can't be me. Maybe the Buddha didn't know everything." Doubt is an insidious enemy—doubt in the Buddha, the Dhamma, the Sangha, in the teacher, one's own abilities, the instructions, or even the whole concept of the teaching. These doubts make it not just hard but impossible to meditate, because the mind is too busy with needless concerns. If we want to meditate, we have to let go of all that kind of thinking.

We also have to drop the idea of perfection, the tightness of wanting; in fact, we have to drop all ideas and just be there. Doubt makes it very difficult to have complete commitment and dedication to the spiritual path, and without these the path will be stony indeed. Doubt makes us go from one teaching to another and makes us unable to commit ourselves to any of them. Again and again we abandon what we have begun and try out something new. To be committed means to give ourselves fully, and to do this we need to have found confidence within our own hearts.

Skeptical doubt, the Buddha said, is like traveling through the desert with very little food and no road map and being in great danger throughout the long journey. Our uncertainty about what might be helpful to us, what path we should follow, often prevents our doing the necessary practice, although we would find that through practice our understanding deepens. Meditation helps the mind to become malleable, flexible, pliable, and because of this, it is capable of knowing far more.

Doubt is not to be confused with investigation. It is important to try to find our own relationship to what is being taught: "How does this affect me? What can I actually do to realize the truth?" Also, doubt is not the opposite of belief. The Buddha never advocated unquestioning belief but wanted us to develop enough confidence in what he said to enable us to practice free from the burden of constant doubts.

In another sutta, he speaks about the prerequisites for the practice of meditation. The first is to know our own dukkha, to recognize where it comes from, and how it operates within our own lives. The second is to gain confidence in the teaching, to realize that we can actually take this path. The third is to experience joy at the opportunity we have been given. Only when all three are present will meditation bear fruit. This joy is not a typical worldly joy, though joyful gratitude for all that we have, or simply the joy of seeing a beautiful view, or a flower, can certainly be helpful. Inner joy, however, arises from knowing that we have found a wonderful teaching, based on the highest ideal, and that we are attempting to draw nearer and nearer to it. It is this that will help us to meditate. If we sit down with the idea, "Oh dear, another meditation session, I suppose I must stick it out," we will never be able to do it. There must be a feeling of strength and uplift in the mind. Meditation will enhance both, but we have to bring them with us in the first place.

Every human being experiences all five of the hindrances, but each of us will find that one particular hindrance gives us more trouble than the others. It is worthwhile finding out which this might be. If sloth and torpor are the particular enemies, then we arouse the perception of light. If it is ill-will, we arouse loving-kindness. With sensual desire, we recognize the dukkha this brings us and try to let go. Should it be restlessness and worry, we see that it is connected to not having what we want and try to drop the desire. We understand that restlessness is concerned with our self-image, our wish to have a certain standing in the world, to be appreciated, and that this is an unnecessary endeavor. It is quite difficult to get this particular recognition, since everybody else is also working hard to get it for themselves.

Letting go of the hindrances does not mean that they will be uprooted and disappear forever. We can think of them as weeds in our garden. If we keep cutting down the weeds, we weaken the roots, and they no longer have the strength they had, nor do they any longer overshadow the good plants. We can only completely uproot the hindrances when we have gained sufficient inner strength to do so. Meanwhile, we work at cutting them down. At the beginning of each meditation, we ask ourselves: "Am I having thoughts of ill-will? Doubt? Restlessness and worry? Am I feeling lazy and sleepy? Is my mind filled with desires?" If so, we try to drop these obstacles, using the antidotes of loving-kindness and of calming the mind, remembering that there is nothing to gain and everything to get rid of.

# 4

## The First Meditative Absorption

Having dealt with all the preliminary steps leading to concentrated meditation, the sutta now comes to the first meditative absorption, or *jhāna*. At this point it might be useful to say that anyone who reads the discourses of the Buddha as transmitted to us in the Pali Canon, on which Theravāda tradition bases its teaching, cannot help but see that the meditative absorptions are a part of the path. As with the other teachings we have heard so far in this sutta—the five hindrances, guarding of the senses, mindfulness, and clear comprehension—all are steps on the same pathway. If we really want a spiritual teaching that will bring us joy and happiness, we need every part of it. We cannot pick and choose, a bit here, a bit there, simply because we find something difficult or someone has told us it is not necessary. These are only personal views and opinions. The Buddha was able to show the whole path, and it is much safer and far more productive to adhere to what he said. This is not the only discourse that mentions the meditative absorptions; there are dozens of them. I am stressing this point because it is not uncommon for meditators to accidentally touch upon the meditative absorptions and not know what they are experiencing. Many have tried unsuccessfully to find some guidance. Having read what the Buddha says in the suttas, it is possible to try to follow his teaching on one's own, but it is not easy. Most of us need help.

Now let us look at the Buddha's teaching on the jhānas in this discourse. He says: "when he [the monk] knows that the five hindrances have left him...." This is very important. The five hindrances are temporarily eliminated in the first jhāna. They have no chance of arising during the meditative absorptions, but we have to actually sit down without them. Since they still exist within us, we must not allow them to arise. We can see that we have to start out with love and compassion, without any doubts, without any sensual desire, without sloth and torpor, or ill-will, or restlessness and worry. The hindrances have to be put aside at the time of meditation. In fact this is something we naturally aim for. If any of the hindrances arise, the mind immediately becomes agitated, then there is no way we can meditate. However, if we sit down with loving-kindness, compassion, and contentment, and with the determination to concentrate, though without any thought of a result, the hindrances are quite blocked. Meditation should bring some feelings of being at ease, because when the five hindrances are absent even temporarily, we feel quite peaceful.

> And when he knows that these five hindrances have left him, gladness arises in him, from gladness comes delight, from the delight in his mind his body is tranquilized...

Here gladness and delight are still on a worldly level, not yet on a meditative level. In Pali, there are several different words to describe this, but in English we are more limited. "Gladness" is a feeling of ease and well-being, and with this, the body becomes stable. With a tranquil body, we feel joy, and with joy in the mind, we become concentrated. This should never be forgotten by anyone who wishes to meditate. Joy or delight in the mind is a necessary prerequisite; without it, meditation has no chance.

Here delight is described as being a result of a stable and tranquil body. This feeling of stability and tranquility arises from a mind that is glad to meditate. Joy may come from different causes; there is joy in knowing we can actually follow a path, joy in sitting quietly, joy that there is well-being in the body. If we do not have such joy, particularly joy in our spiritual practice, meditation will fall by the wayside whenever it seems to us that we have something more important to do.

Without joy, there is no concentration. We hardly ever hear this mentioned, though the Buddha refers to it often. He says that we can only meditate if we feel comfortable in body and mind, and we can only concentrate if the mind is joyful. If we really know why we are practicing and truly appreciate our own efforts, that understanding alone brings joy.

This is still *pamojja*, "worldly joy," not yet *sukha*, or "meditative joy." But when we are able to sit down without the five hindrances, the whole mind and body system of which we consist feels tranquilized, as if it were being pulled together. We sense we are beginning something that has the greatest potential we have ever come across.

The Buddha continues:

> Being thus detached from sense-desires, detached from
> unwholesome states, he enters and remains in the first jhāna...

The word "detached" is frequently misunderstood because the texts do not always specify "detached from sense desires and unwholesome states." Some suttas simply say that the first jhāna is entered through detachment. This is then taken to mean that we should remove ourselves from our ordinary way of life and perhaps go live in the forest for an extended time. It can be helpful to live in the forest, but it is not necessary. "Detachment" means nothing more than having, at that time, no sense desires or unwholesome states, which is simply once again the need to set aside the five hindrances. The result is a feeling of lightening the burden.

> ...he enters and remains in the first jhāna, which is with
> thinking and pondering...

Unfortunately, the Pali words *vitakka-vicāra* are often translated as "thinking and pondering." All meditators know that if they think and ponder, they cannot get into first jhāna. But *vitakka-vicāra* have a second meaning, namely "initial and sustained application to the meditation subject," and that is what is being referred to here.

"...[B]orn of detachment, filled with delight and joy." Now we come to the meditative aspect of delight and joy. They both arise simultaneously. Delight in this instance is a delightful sensation, and joy comes with it. This time it is called *sukha*. We will see later that it is the main aspect of the second meditative absorption. In the first jhāna this delightful sensation manifests itself in many different ways and strengths. It can be overwhelming or quite mild. It can be a feeling of lightness, floating, rising up, expansion, extension, tingling—any one of these and others, but always delightful.

This state is also translated as "interest," meaning we become vitally interested in meditation. If we stay with the breath at this time, we are missing the boat. Whatever methods we use, they are nothing more than a key to put in the keyhole, unlock the door, and step over the threshold to get inside, where we become acquainted with our true inner life. We will discover that everything we are carrying around in our minds is nothing but extraneous matter. It has been put there by our desires, rejections, reactions, thoughts, plans, hopes, ideas, and viewpoints. As we become concentrated enough to enter into our inner being and experience delightful sensations, we can actually realize this truth.

We also need to know that these sensations are always with us. We are not making them appear. That would be quite a feat. They are always there, but we are not able to get in touch with them because of all the turmoil in our minds and hearts. When we acquire the ability to experience those sensations whenever we wish, much of our sensual desire and craving disappears. We realize that we already have what we were craving, and that this is independent of any outer circumstances. We are no longer constantly trying to make everything happen in accordance with our own wishes, which in any case is a futile task.

The experience of first jhāna should make an enormous difference in our lives. However, if we do not continue with regular meditation practice, we do not get to that state often enough and cannot gain insight from it. Even though the sensation may be strong, we do not relate to it in the proper way.

> And with this delight and joy born of detachment, he so suffuses, drenches, fills and irradiates his body that there is no spot in his entire body that is untouched by this delight and joy born of detachment.

If we only feel this delight in some small spot, we must enlarge it. The whole body should be "suffused and drenched" with it. What is being spoken of is a bodily sensation, though not the kind that we are familiar with in ordinary daily living. It is similar to exceedingly pleasant sense contact, but not the same. It is far more subtle and far more satisfying, and we can be, so to speak, in charge of it. Once we have learned to concentrate, we can get to the delightful sensation any time we wish and stay in it as long as we wish. Anyone who becomes a master of the jhānas can do this. They can also go from any of the eight jhānas to any other, not necessarily in sequence, leaving and entering them whenever they choose. But that of course is at a later stage.

Having reached the first jhāna, he remains in it. And whatever sensations of lust that he previously had disappear. At that time there is present a true but subtle perception of delight and happiness....

The first thing we learn here is that lust disappears. Clearly, at a time when we are experiencing delightful sensations in the body, lust will not arise. We are already contented with what we have. It can, of course, still arise at other times, but the more insight we get from the meditative path, and the more we develop the ability to get into the jhānas, the less danger there is of that happening.

The word "lust" usually means "sexual desire," which is our strongest sensual desire, and which therefore plays havoc with many people's lives. Strong passions can be extremely tumultuous, so having a remedy can be of the utmost importance. Here we are only addressing the period of time spent in the jhāna. However, as insight arises and we realize that all we are craving for already exists within us, and prove this to ourselves over and over again, we have a great chance of letting go of lust—if not completely, at any rate to such an extent that it no longer bothers us.

...a true but subtle perception of delight and happiness...

"True" means that we are actually experiencing it. The word "subtle" is used to describe the first four jhānas, which are known as the fine, or subtle-form jhānas. In worldly life, we do in fact experience similar states, but they are far more gross. We can have delightful sensations, but they are always dependent on outside causes. We cannot arrange for them to happen when we choose. Usually, once they are over, the feeling of satisfaction and contentment leaves us. That does not happen in the jhānas. Because of their subtle nature, the satisfaction remains. Also, we know we can enter into them at any time we want. We will see, as we progress to the second, third, and fourth jhānas, that their subtle sensations have an equivalent in our ordinary experiences, but only at a gross and ultimately unsatisfactory level. They are short-lived, and we may not be able to repeat them at will. Whereas in the jhānas, all we need to do to repeat the experience is sit down and concentrate.

Being concentrated in this way is of great benefit to the mind because it eliminates discursive thinking. All our hopes, plans, worries, fears, likes, and dislikes are set aside. It is the one way of being truly at ease, and we can do nothing better for ourselves.

"... [A]nd he becomes one who is conscious of this delight and happiness...." In other words, he puts his attention on it. "'In this way, some perceptions arise through training, and some pass away through training. And this is that training,' said the Lord."

If you remember, Poṭṭhapāda asked the Buddha about the extinction of higher consciousness and wanted to know how consciousness arises and how one becomes "unconscious." He had heard of four different ways in which that could happen. But the Buddha told him they were all quite inaccurate. "One's perceptions arise and cease," he said, "owing to a cause and conditions. Some perceptions arise through training and some pass away through training." He then gave Poṭṭhapāda details of the training through which the mind becomes so purified that it can get into the first jhāna. In that state, he said, the subtle perception of delight and happiness arises, and it ceases when the mind leaves the jhāna. This was the first part of his answer to Poṭṭhapāda's question.

The Buddha then gives a simile for how it feels to experience the first jhāna. This is also interesting from a historical point of view as it shows us how soap was made in those days.

> Just as a skilled bathman or his assistant, kneading the soap powder which he has sprinkled with water, forms from it, in a metal dish, a soft lump, so that the ball of soap-powder becomes one oleaginous mass, bound with oil so that nothing escapes, so this monk suffuses, drenches, fills and irradiates his body so that no spot remains untouched.

A delightful explanation how first jhāna should be experienced, all over the body. It is vital to remember that when we sit down to meditate, none of the hindrances should be present. In order for this to be possible, we need to watch the mind during our ordinary activities outside of the meditation period. We should have mindfulness of thought-content, not allowing the mind to race around continually in search of ways to fulfill our desires.

We should remain mindful and constantly attentive to our physical actions, voluntary or impulsive. In this way, the mind will already have made a start at ridding itself of the hindrances.

If the mind is capable of sitting down without the presence of the hindrances, then there is absolutely no reason why we should not become concentrated. But as soon as it thinks, "I want to be concentrated; I ought to be able to do it; perhaps I should try some other way," then of course all our efforts are spoiled. We should simply let ourselves "be," without those constant ideas, those intervening difficulties. None of them have any real truth in them; they are all human-made, mind-made. The truth looks entirely different, and we get nearer to it through the meditative states. Of course there is more to be done, but at least we are elevating the mind to a level where we realize "there is a consciousness within me other than the one I know."

At the end of any jhāna, indeed at the end of any good meditation, we should do three things. The first is to realize that as one comes out of the meditation, the pleasant state dissolves. One should watch it dissolve and recognize that it, too, is impermanent. Do not just say this mechanically—some of us have heard and used the word "impermanent" so often that we hardly know what it means any more. We simply agree that everything is impermanent. Really watch the desirable state disappear. It is not the letter, but the spirit of the teaching that matters, and that means experiencing for ourselves. We can read a thousand books, repeat a thousand verses, all in vain. Wisdom comes only from the understood experience and from nothing else.

Everyone has experiences constantly. If we understood them correctly, we would already be enlightened. We all, for instance, experience the impermanence of each breath, and yet many of us continue to entertain myriad ideas about our future. We have not understood the experience, that there is only this moment. There is no future, there is no past. Everything is now, and we are completely transparent; we have no solidity. We only look as if we had.

We are all aware of the impermanence of our thoughts, that they arise, unasked, and disappear. In fact, we would rather they did not arise, for we would prefer to be concentrated. Yet we believe that "This is me, thinking. These are my thoughts." We should investigate this belief. Usually when we own something, we have some jurisdiction over it. Yet the thoughts that are occurring now, and all the others that we "owned" in the past have gone, have they not? Where is the "I" who owned them? Gone too? Or is it constantly "owning" new ones? But which is the real "I" then? Is it the one we had before, or the one we have now? What happens to that "I" every time a new thought disappears? There may well be a gap between one thought and the next; that does happen. Where is the "I" then? Is it taking a holiday? How are we going to get it back? Why, by thinking, of course!

The misunderstood experience is the cause of our "me" illusion. The first thing to do after coming out of the jhāna is to recognize its impermanence and, possibly at the same time, become aware of the impermanence of thoughts, emotions, breath, the whole body.

The next thing to be done after the meditation is to recapitulate. How did I arrive at the concentrated state of mind? What was the method? No method has, in itself, any intrinsic value. The one that works for you is the one to use. It very often happens that people get attached to a particular method, and because it has been successful for them, they think everyone else should use it too. This is a mistake. Our underlying tendencies vary slightly. One method may suit one person better than another. For instance, it may be very helpful to use the loving-kindness meditation as a way of getting concentrated. In this meditation, if we do it well, a strong feeling arises, usually in the center of the chest. This is commonly a very pleasant physical feeling of warmth. Sometimes it is a feeling of both warmth and joy. As soon as it arises, rather than continuing with the loving-kindness meditation, we should put our full attention on the sensation itself. The stronger sensation will be the physical one, so that is where our attention should go first.

It makes no difference how we manage to concentrate, just so long as we do. Then we can truthfully say, "I am meditating." Until then, all we can say is we are using a meditation method. This distinction is hardly ever made, though it is clearly pointed out by the Buddha.

Some people come to it through the "sweeping exercise," particularly if they use the fan method.[2] If done correctly, it may bring enough concentration to arouse a very pleasant sensation. If that should be the case, then we stop the sweeping right then and there and put our attention on the delightful sensation. Then, as we have heard from the Buddha, we enlarge the sensation so that it is experienced throughout the body.

Another method are the *kasinas*, the color disks. If we are visually inclined and find it easy to conjure up a color, then we may be able to see a round color disk, enlarge it, and be totally immersed in it. This too leads to the first jhāna and is the purpose of the kasina meditation.

Or, as we stay on the breath, and it becomes very fine, a bright light may appear. This too can be enlarged so that it surrounds us completely. Once we have stayed within this light for some time, it will not only surround us, but become extremely pleasant as the delightful sensation arises.

As we can see, there are many possibilities, though it would certainly not be useful to try them all out in one sitting. However, if we feel that loving-kindness meditation works very well for us, then we should use it as our way to become concentrated. Or, if we spontaneously see colors, and they arise to the point where we find it difficult to watch the breath because they are in the way, then we should use the colors. If we become very concentrated when doing the sweeping exercise, we use that. The method does not matter. All that matters is that we sit down with joyful understanding of the great potential that lies within us.

Everyone who possesses patience and perseverance can get to the jhānas. It is a natural way for the mind to go. In fact, almost everyone who comes to meditation has that underlying yearning. They may not know what the word "jhāna" means, or what a meditative absorption is, but that is not important. Our inner yearning is a longing for relief and release from the thinking mind. Sometimes that yearning is unconscious, but often it is already acknowledged and understood, as if there were some kind of intuition that such a thing is possible. When an unprejudiced person hears of the jhānas for the first time, the mind usually says: "Aha! I knew there was something!"

Sometimes, when we experience a jhāna for the first time, we remember that we did this as a child. This is more common than we might imagine. Small children often do it spontaneously. In the process of growing up, as schooling, family, and sex all intervene, then such things are forgotten. But should we, after much dukkha, come to meditation in adult life and reach first jhāna, then the memory returns.

The Buddha, while he was still the Bodhisattva, Prince Siddhartha Gotama, left the palace and his family to go into the forest to study meditation. He learned the first seven jhānas from one teacher, and immediately on entering the first, he remembered that he had already done so when he was twelve years old.

The story of how that happened concerns his father, King Suddhodana, who ruled over a minor kingdom. It was the tradition there that when spring came, the season of rice planting, the king should turn the first sod. King Suddhodana took his twelve year-old son with him, and the boy was supposed to hold one handle of the plough while his father held the other, and thus they would turn the first sod together. But when the time came, the boy was nowhere to be found. The king sent one of his ministers to look for him. He was discovered sitting under a tree, obviously meditating and totally transported. Not liking to disturb him, the minister reported back to the king, who said he would turn the sod by himself.

Later, between the ages of twelve and twenty-nine, the prince indulged in all forms of sensual gratification. He also married and had a son. Finally, however, he decided that the suffering of humankind must be addressed and went to the forest to learn meditation. It was easy for him to enter the jhānas because of his previous experiences in past lives and as a young boy in this life. This may not be true for everyone, but it seems that people who have had that kind of childhood experience do enter the jhānas with greater ease. The rest of us may have to work a little harder, but that will be a lesson in patience and perseverance.

Contrary to what is sometimes said, the experience of the first jhāna does not produce attachment. The Buddha never mentioned such a possibility. The idea first arose in later commentaries written hundreds of years after the Buddha's death.

Far from producing attachment, the experience leads to a certain vigor and the urgency to "get on with it," because we are then able to see the enormous difference between worldly and jhāna mind-states. Even if the feeling of urgency does not arise, the understanding that "this cannot be all" is certain to surface. Every intelligent person recognizes immediately that the goal of meditation cannot simply be to have a delightful sensation. Happy though we may be to have such a feeling, we instinctively know that there must be more to it than that and are very much interested in continuing.

The fact that the mind is pure and translucent at that time, however, makes it a very important happening. Purity of mind is one of the greatest boons of the jhānas. That purity has two aspects. First, there is no obstruction, no hindrance; none of our defilements are present. Secondly, it brings clarity. When something is pure, it becomes clear. When a window is dirty, it is hard to look out, but when it is polished, we can see clearly. Clarity of mind is what we need for insight.

Purity of mind comes from diligent, continual practice. It comes from knowing ourselves and recognizing what needs to be done. We have already looked at these preliminary stages, which are mentioned in this sutta.

Clarity is what we are really after, because it gives us the ability to understand our experiences. As we acquire this clarity, we will obviously take great care not to refill our minds with impurity. We will constantly be on guard. This is because we now realize what a jewel we have; a mind whose purity and clarity can break through all delusions and see the world in its absolute truth.

In order to gain the depth and profundity of insight taught by the Buddha, we need such a state of mind. It can only come about if we are able to stay totally focused, without any discursive thinking. As long as there are thoughts, we are on the worldly level, and we will only know what is already in our minds.

The third step after the meditation is to contemplate the *jhānic* experience to become aware of any newly arisen insight. Such insights are particularly illuminating as they come from our own personal understanding. The Buddha was a very pragmatic teacher, and when he taught the first four meditative absorptions, he simply numbered them. This is in fact very helpful because it means that there is no need to imagine anything. We simply carry out his instructions. Those numbered five to eight were given names, and we shall be looking at these too.

These states of consciousness are the natural way for the mind to go. We can read of them in the reports written by Christian and other mystics. The terminology may be different, but not the experience. Teresa of Avila, giving instructions to her nuns in her book *Interior Castle*, described seven of the meditative absorptions, though in such a visionary way that today hardly anybody can follow her. The descriptions are so elaborate that the reader has the impression that the experience was a purely personal one. The Buddha's explanations, on the contrary, are pragmatic, so that there is no possibility of making that mistake. It is obvious that they are for everyone.

Other Christian mystics, such as Meister Eckhart and Francisco de Osuna, also practiced the absorptions, though their descriptions of them are again different.

Because we are living in an age where technology, not religion, is at the helm, the absorptions are becoming a lost art. But there is no need for them to become lost; they can be revived, for we are in the lucky position of having the Buddha's words available to us.

Since some people touch upon the absorptions quite spontaneously, without guidance or instruction, we can infer that this is a natural result of one-pointedness. There are those who have done it in moments of great joy, others in times of great stress. This is not uncommon. Others arrive at it simply by becoming concentrated.

Meditation is the science of the mind. Because it is a science, it is explainable and repeatable, but it has to include all possible dimensions. We are all familiar with the dimensions of the worldly mind; the one that thinks, judges, is happy or unhappy, that wants or does not want. It is always in a state of duality, in which "we" are opposed to "the world." If meditation does not bring a different experience, it cannot bring satisfaction.

The elevated consciousness, which we experience through meditation, shows us clearly that we are in this world, but not of it. We learn that we can in fact transcend it, while remaining in this body and mind. That is why the Buddha guided everyone through the jhānas to the insights. In any discourse that encompasses the whole path, beginning with morality and ending with enlightenment, the jhānas are never left out. One word of warning: we must not sit down to meditate with the intention of reaching a delightful sensation. Instead, we simply follow the method we have chosen, the one we feel is best for us, and stay with it. That is all that is necessary.

# 5

# The Second and Third
# Meditative Absorptions

The path the Buddha taught and is explaining to Poṭṭhapāda in this sutta has to be followed step by step. First comes morality, then guarding the sense-doors, mindfulness and clear comprehension, contentment, letting go of the hindrances, and—only after these—the first meditative absorption. It is like a road map, which will take us from one point to the next on our journey. Everyone knows how to use a map. If we do not follow the signs, we get lost. In order to drive from, say, Los Angeles to New York, it is no use only looking at a map of New York. We need one that guides us every mile of the road, each step on the way to our destination.

Having described the first meditative absorption, the Buddha now speaks of the second jhāna. In the following translation, "initial and sustained application" can be substituted for "thinking and pondering."

> Again, a monk, with the subsiding of thinking and pondering by gaining inner tranquillity and unity of mind, reaches and remains in the second jhāna, which is free from thinking and pondering, born of concentration, filled with delight and happiness.

Initially we applied the mind to watching the breath and then sustained that attention. There is no further need for this now. Reaching the first jhāna has concentrated the mind sufficiently, so that it remains steady. However, this does not hold true early on; it only comes with practice. In the beginning, the mind wavers and falls off the meditation subject, and we may have to repeat the initial and sustained application. Practically speaking, it seems that the delightful sensation we were concentrated on dissolves while we are still trying to stay on it. In fact, however, our concentration disappears. The sensation is always there; we did not create it. We may find that, instead of starting again with the breath, or the loving-kindness meditation, or whatever subject we have chosen, we are able simply to put the mind back on the sensation. Having noticed the place in the body where the sensation is strongest, we return to that spot. It is not that we put the attention on the body itself. We put it on the delightful sensation, but since it is housed in the body, we find that place. If we are not able to do this, we may have to go back to the initial and sustained application. It depends upon our degree of concentration.

When we are practiced enough, we get to the second jhāna by voluntarily dropping our concentration on the delightful sensation. We do this when we have stayed on it for a sufficient length of time, totally immersed in it, completely cognizant of it. Ten to fifteen minutes is more than enough, but it must be unwavering. When we let go of our concentration on the delightful sensation, it must be on purpose. In another sutta, the Buddha says since we know that the physical delight and the bodily sensations are still gross, we therefore look for the next, higher stage, which are the emotions.

Once we have let go of the delightful sensation, we focus on the inner joy, which is present at that time. Because it is already there, we just need to change our focus of attention. In this sutta it is not called joy, but delight and happiness. The delight remains in the background of our awareness. There is still lightness of body and a loss of bodily feeling as if there were no gravity. If we are concentrated enough, there should be no physical discomfort, no pain anywhere, though it may return when we come out of the jhāna. Joy now comes to the foreground. This is the meditative joy, *sukha*, and it is the one that really tranquilizes because it is the antidote for restlessness and worry. If we are experiencing any difficulty in going to this inner joy, it is sometimes helpful to say the word "joy" softly to ourselves. When we put our mind on the word, that is where our whole being goes. This does not work for everyone. Some may find it disturbs their concentration.

Both delight and joy still contain an element of excitement. We have the feeling that they are taking place somewhere around the head, which of course is only an impression. When we initially reach the first jhāna, the excitement can be very strong because the mind has all sorts of things to say about the experience. But if we habitually practice the jhānas, that initial excitement disappears completely. A very subtle excitement, however, will remain. We are not yet really tranquil, but we have to go through each stage, step by step, for each is cause and effect. The effect of a delightful sensation is caused by our concentration. The delight causes the feeling of joy, for how could we not be joyful if we experience such delight? Most people have no experience of this inner joy because for them joy will always be dependent on an outer sense-contact. We can gain a great deal of insight from getting in touch with our inner joy.

> His former true but subtle perception of delight and happiness born of detachment vanishes. At that time there arises a true but subtle perception of delight and happiness born of concentration, and he becomes one who is conscious of this delight and happiness. In this way, some perceptions arise through training, and some pass away through training.

The word "perception" is chosen in this text, but the word "consciousness" applies equally well. The sutta is also called *States of Consciousness*. Here the Buddha is saying that some consciousness arises through training and some passes away through training. We all know what ordinary consciousness or awareness implies. It is sometimes pleasant, sometimes not. It is often connected to wanting something we do not have, or getting rid of something we do have. Because of this, we never have an inner feeling of complete peace and joy. We may not be aware that this is what we truly want, but in fact it is.

The everyday kind of consciousness—the one we all use, for making a living, for relating to each other—is in a state of permanent duality. It is "me" wanting something, "me" opposed to the world, "me" opposed to you. "I" remain outside of everything, which is not conducive to peacefulness.

We are all familiar with these mind-states. Most people in the world think they are all there is. Because of that belief, they quite logically look to the outer world in their search for pleasure and happiness. But when we start to meditate, we realize that a totally different consciousness may become available to us. In the first instance, this has a great impact. Later it becomes something we deeply know. As we practice, great compassion arises because of our awareness of these other states of consciousness. The difference between our everyday consciousness and the elevated states is so immense that we cannot but feel enormous compassion, and from that comes the desire to help. This is what the Buddha did, from the day of his enlightenment at the age of thirty-five to the day of his death at the age of eighty. In the scriptures it says that he taught every day, even in inclement weather, even when his health was bad. He always walked to wherever he was to teach, however long the distance. In his day, the only transport was by ox- or horse-cart, and he did not want to give his weight to an animal to pull, so he went on foot. It is still a rule for monks and nuns not to travel by animal-drawn cart, in case it causes suffering. The scriptures also say that he meditated every morning and "threw out the net of his compassion." Symbolically this means that he used his clairvoyance to "catch" anyone who might be ready to listen. He said that there were only a few people "with little dust in their eyes," and he would go out of his way to reach them, knowing that they were open to the truth of the Dhamma.

In the first jhāna, there is "a true but subtle perception of delight and happiness, born of detachment." That is to say, detachment from our sense desires, hindrances, or any unwholesome states. Then, in the second jhāna, there is delight and happiness "born of concentration." This means that our concentration will have deepened. It is not uncommon for wispy, fleeting thoughts to arise in the first jhāna. We will also still hear sounds, though not as clearly as we do in everyday life—they will be a little removed. In the second jhāna they become further removed, as if we were sitting under a glass dome, which mutes them and renders them much less disturbing. Our concentration grows stronger, and as we progress through the jhānas, it will become increasingly one-pointed.

Such concentration brings purification, and with purification comes clarity. One leads to the other. The Buddha's teaching is sometimes called the teaching of cause and effect because his clear and unequivocal guidelines lead us step by step, each being the cause for the arising of the next. We can easily realize this intellectually, and that is always the starting point—understanding the teaching. This will not initially bring us calm or insight, but without it we will be unable to progress. Understanding engages our mind, but it must be accompanied by an opening of the heart. If that does not happen, all the understanding in the world cannot help us. We may sound impressive when we talk of the teaching, we may even write learned books about it, but we will never be able to free ourselves from our own dukkha. If the heart does not open, the vision of the Dhamma cannot enter. Confidence in the teaching, born of understanding, leads to joy in practice. Heart and mind should always work together.

On leaving a jhāna, or any good meditation, we know already that there are three steps to be taken. The first is to recognize the impermanence of the experience, and the second is to remember the pathway we used to reach concentration. Now we will discuss some details of the third step, when we ask ourselves: "What have I learned from this experience; what insight have I gained?"

In reaching the delightful sensation of first jhāna, the mind immediately recognizes an elevated, expanded consciousness, one that is far removed from the marketplace mentality of wanting to get something, or get rid of something else. This expansion of consciousness gives rise to an understanding that there is more to life than the senses. Even the most pleasing and subtle sense-contacts, such as flowers, rainbows, sunsets, and poems, which have absolutely no trace of unwholesomeness, are external to us, and we are dependent on their pleasing aspects for our happiness. However, they do not always give us delight. We may believe that it is the quality of the sunset that is giving us such pleasure, but in fact it is the quality of our own immersion in the sunset that brings the delight. Often we think the pleasure comes from the outside, but the particular sensual experience is only the trigger through which we may become so totally focused that we lose all sense of a "me." At that point there is no one around to say, "I want it; I want to keep it." But once the sunset is over and the delight has vanished, the "me" returns, and with it the idea that "I" should go looking for other sunsets because they bring such pleasure. This is an illustration of the fact that we experience everything we need to reach enlightenment, but we do not quite understand our experiences. We need the Dhamma to guide us, and then we can see things as they really are.

Our first understanding, or insight, is that there exists a different level of consciousness, and that we can experience delight that is within, not external to us. It is our own purity and concentration that allow us to experience it. From this we can infer that everything we have ever looked for is already within. Most people look for satisfaction, happiness, and joy outside of themselves and do not even recognize that sense-contacts are always dependent on the exterior world and never reliable.

When we come to the joy experienced in the second jhāna, we realize that it is of a far finer quality than any joy we have ever known before. Also it is quite independent of external conditions. Our whole being is suffused with joy in a way that is not possible through sense-contacts. Knowing that we are able to do this brings with it a second insight—that there is no longer any necessity to be constantly looking for pleasant sense-contacts, though they will of course still occur. This makes an enormous difference to our lives. The search for pleasure through the senses involves a great expenditure of time and energy and is linked to dukkha because either we cannot get what we want, or only partially, or someone stands in our way.

This second step on the path of the jhānas brings about a huge change in our habits, as we automatically integrate the experience into our daily life. Our senses are still what they always were. Our eyes see, our ears hear, we can taste, touch, smell, think, but we do not have to go to such endless trouble searching for pleasurable contacts.

On the contrary, it quite often happens during longer meditation courses that people find the green in nature suddenly much greener and the sky much bluer. Neither the sky nor the foliage, of course, have changed; it is the perception that has become clearer. This clarity is due to the fact that at that time we are not looking for pleasures through the senses, or wanting to hold on to them, or repeat them. The pleasure is simply there, without any tinge of desire. Ordinarily we never even notice the dukkha that accompanies pleasure, the dukkha of attachment, of "wanting to keep." But what we have here is a straightforward sense-contact, which has a more refined quality. This too is a result of the realization that we do not have to look to the outer world for what is already within us.

The peace of mind that comes from that is not yet absolute, but it certainly brings a sense of tranquility to our everyday lives. We know it is all available within; we do not have to "do" anything or go anywhere. Naturally we will still do things. In fact, we will usually do them much better because we are not so attached to the result, or more precisely, to the idea that our happiness depends on that result. We simply do, because something needs to be done. In consequence, we do it more easily, without any inner tension. We know there is something else more refined, subtler, greater than what happens on the worldly level. Not that we start despising the world or rejecting it. It is simply that we no longer have the same expectation of it. Where there is no expectation, there is no disappointment. Everything begins to fall into place on a very peaceful level.

The Buddha says of the second jhāna (in the *Sāmaññaphala Sutta*):

> And with this delight and joy born of concentration he so suffuses his body that no spot remains untouched.

We must not misunderstand how this happens. The delight and joy are mental concomitants, but they appear to manifest in the body. For instance, we may say that we experience joy in the middle of the chest, which is the home of the spiritual heart. The joy is a mental and emotional state, but we point to a spot in the body. This is quite natural, for we have no way of experiencing anything except through our mind-body connection. In the second jhāna we use the delight, which is in the background, and the joy, which is in the foreground, to suffuse ourselves from top to bottom. We often say in the loving-kindness meditation that we should "fill ourselves with joy from head to toe." If we are able to do this in the loving-kindness meditation, it provides an entry to the jhānas.

As with the first jhāna, the Buddha also gives a simile for the second:

> Just as a lake fed by a spring, with no inflow from east, west, north or south, where the rain-god sends moderate showers from time to time, the water welling up from below, mingling with cool water, would suffuse, fill and irradiate that cool water, so that no part of the pool was untouched by it—so with this delight and joy born of concentration, he so suffuses his body that no spot remains untouched.

This is a very useful instruction because often joy is felt only in the chest area. But we can quite easily enlarge upon that, so that we feel joy everywhere within us. Then, and only then, do we experience the completeness of the second jhāna. When we are totally suffused by it, it has a quality that no joy we have known before has ever had. There is a sweetness about it, a sense of fulfillment, and because of this, our mind-states change. The experience of inner joy brings with it self-confidence because we realize that we can be happy quite independent of outer conditions. This creates a sense of freedom, which gives rise to honesty and self-reliance. Now we are able to take the next step and enter the third jhāna.

Due to that fulfillment in joy, which is the antidote for our restlessness and worry, contentment arises. This is not the kind of contentment mentioned earlier where, in order to start our meditation, we need to feel content with our situation and with who we are, grateful for what is good in our lives, at ease and satisfied. For that, we have to deliberately recall those features of our lives and put our attention on them. Here the contentment is of a different quality. It arises because we experience what we have always wanted—fulfilling joy.

After a certain length of time we can and should let go of the joy, even though we find it most delightful, and allow the mind to immerse itself in contentment. We will have the feeling that the mind drops down. Not that it does any such thing, of course, but that is how it might feel. The first two jhānas seem to be happening in an upper region around the head, whereas the third has a feeling of more depth.

This is what the Buddha says about the third jhāna:

> Again, after the fading away of delight he dwells in equanimity, mindful and clearly aware, and he experiences in his body that pleasant feeling of which the Noble Ones say: "Happy dwells the one of equanimity and mindfulness, and he reaches and remains in the third jhāna."

In this passage it is called "equanimity." That is, in fact, a feature of the fourth jhāna, so it is often difficult to distinguish between the third and fourth. Practically speaking, however, it can be done in the following manner: First, we let go of the joy. We do this deliberately, not because our concentration has waned. Should that happen, the whole meditation usually comes to a halt. It is much better practice to let go on purpose after having been totally immersed. In another discourse the Buddha says that in realizing that the joy, the emotional state, is still quite gross, one reaches for a finer, more subtle, and higher state.

Some people find it difficult to let the joy go. Others have difficulty in finding it in the first place. There are all sorts of obstacles, but eventually we can learn the whole pathway. There is no reason, none whatsoever, why we should not be able to train our minds. It is a matter of patience and perseverance, and of not thinking about results. The achievement syndrome has to be left behind. There is nothing to achieve; it is all there already.

We let go of inner joy by no longer putting our attention on it; once we do this, it disappears. We realize this is another example of the truth that we can only be aware of what we put our mind on. The mind is at ease and contented now. The first thing we experience is a feeling of peacefulness and tranquility. The word "equanimity" is really quite descriptive because contentment is equanimity. "Mindful and clearly aware" is a description of the mind's one-pointedness; it is totally aware and awake. The "pleasant feeling" that is mentioned is a feature of any jhāna. They are all utterly pleasant, but here the delightful bodily sensation of the first jhāna and the joy of the second jhāna have been left behind, and in the third jhāna the pleasantness derives from contentment and peacefulness.

This is an important insight, which means the arising of wisdom. The two go hand in hand and can only manifest through our own personal experience. The simile usually given is biting into a mango. If we have never eaten one and want to know what it tastes like, someone may give us a perfectly accurate description. They may, perhaps, even add diagrams and pictures: "That's a mango and that's what it tastes like." But are we any the wiser? We have no clue as to what its taste might be. We can admire the diagrams and descriptions, but we will never know how it tastes until we bite into it ourselves. This is what the Buddha teaches over and over again. But we are very apt to forget this because of the effort involved.

As a result of contentment and peacefulness, another insight may arise. While we are in the jhāna itself, we should not try to understand what is happening because that would involve a thought process. But having had the experience, insights follow automatically. We realize that there can only be contentment and peace, if there is no wish for anything. This makes such an impact that we will undoubtedly try to carry it over into our everyday life. Not that we will always be successful. The mind has every kind of desire, some quite refined, others absurd. But we now know that with every desire we have, we are only hurting ourselves, and that the contentment and peace we experience in the third jhāna is far superior to the fulfillment of any desire. Realizing this, we can very often drop the desire, and by so doing, drop the dukkha—the wanting, the restlessness, the attempts to get and achieve.

Wishlessness is one of the doorways to enlightenment. But how do we do it? Only by experiencing it, at least briefly, can we assess its value. The third jhāna does not, of course, entail enlightenment, but it does bring peace and contentment, which give us a taste of what it is like to be wishless.

Because of this we begin to deal with life in a different way. We may already have been able to refine some of our desires, but now we understand that even the most refined ones create nothing but restlessness. Our own experience of wishlessness has an enormous effect on our ability to let go of dukkha. We finally know what this particular mango tastes like. We do not have to ask anyone; we do not have to look it up in a book. We know what it is to be wishless; it means to be truly contented, and, vice versa, being contented means being wishless.

At the time of the jhāna, wishlessness is easy. It comes to us spontaneously as a result of the joy we have experienced. In daily life it is much more difficult. However, we can always refer back to our experience, especially when we have been able to repeat it at will and it has become part of our daily practice. Then the mind becomes more and more accustomed to this state of consciousness.

Insights are never lost. However, if we gain an insight but do not use it, it recedes to the back of the mind, like a foreign language that we have learned but not practiced. When we hear that language again later, we remember that we actually know it and with a great deal of effort bring it to conscious awareness again. It is the same with an insight. If we do not use it in our daily lives, it lies fallow at the back of our mind. We cannot quite get at it until someone else perhaps mentions it and we realize, "Yes, of course, I too have had that insight." Then we might actually use it more consistently. The important thing about insights is to carry them into our everyday life. We should look at them constantly, mull them over, and see if we can enlarge upon them. Then that foreign language of insight becomes our own.

In Buddhism, it is often said that there are two kinds of language: our everyday language and the language of the Dhamma, which is when we speak from the standpoint of absolute truth. The Buddha does both. He speaks about ordinary, everyday happenings and about absolute truths. We need to be aware of this and know when one or the other is being used. When he talks to us about the jhānas, although he is speaking about elevated consciousness, his language is still on the level of relative truth. It is still "me" experiencing the jhānas. We have not yet come to that terminology that, unless we are able to shift our perception, we will find hard to understand.

> His former true but subtle sense of delight and happiness born of concentration vanishes, and there arises at that time a true but subtle sense of equanimity and happiness, and he becomes one who is conscious of this true but subtle sense of equanimity and happiness. In this way some perceptions arise through training, and some pass away through training.

That last sentence, which recurs throughout the sutta, is always directed at Poṭṭhapāda and his original question: How do perceptions, or consciousness, arise and cease? The Buddha tells him it happens in the progression from one jhāna to the next.

In this passage, "equanimity" is the feeling of contentment. Happiness is an underlying factor, as it is in all but two of the jhānas. When we are contented, we cannot be unhappy. It would be impossible.

The Buddha then gives a simile for the third jhāna:

> Just as if, in a pond of blue, red or white lotuses in which the flowers, born in the water, grown in the water, not growing out of the water, are fed from the water's depths, those blue, red or white lotuses would be suffused with the cool water— so with this joy devoid of delight the monk so suffuses his body that no spot remains untouched.

In both this simile and the previous one, the image is of suffusion. We must fill ourselves from head to toe—with delight and joy in the second jhāna, and here with "joy devoid of delight," or equanimity. "Contentment" and "peacefulness" are perhaps better words, for most people do not really know what equanimity is, but we all have some idea of being contented and at peace. The peacefulness of the third jhāna, however, is far greater than anything we can experience in the world.

The interesting thing is that we all carry this peace within. Everyone has it. Yet there are constant wars—wars going on in ourselves, in our families, in the workplace, quite apart from the wars between nations. But all the time this peace rests within us. We only need to concentrate to find it. It is extraordinary that so few of us realize this. Even when we do meditate, it rarely features in our meditation. Yet experiencing our own inner peacefulness and learning how to return to it again and again is enough to change the whole quality of our lives, and not ours alone. For we all influence each other; we cannot help it. Even if we were to sit by ourselves in a lonely cave, we would still have an influence on the world because of the mental and emotional states that emanate from us. As most of us do not live in lonely caves, our contact with other people certainly affects them. If we emanate peacefulness, others will feel it and may be helped by it. They may also be attracted to it and want to emulate it. Not only that, but there is a universal consciousness, and all of us are part and parcel of it. Within universal consciousness, everything that consciousness can produce exists. If we—one, two, ten, or a hundred of us—have inner peace and are able to sustain it for some length of time and so change the quality of our own lives, then that enters into universal consciousness and will always be accessible, always available. Also, what we produce in our own consciousness returns to us from universal consciousness, like an echo. We can only latch onto what we have already produced within. There is no way in which universal consciousness will give us peacefulness, if we do not have the inner experience that can be touched.

It is not a one-way street: "I'm going to be peaceful and the rest of the world can perish." The Buddha never had a thought of that kind. His whole activity from the day of his enlightenment onward was to show everyone what could be done. Eventually his message spread from country to country. Now it has even come here to us.

In this sutta, the Buddha speaks of "unity of mind," or "one-pointedness," which has a further meaning as well: "unity-consciousness." This consciousness arises very subtly at this point in the jhānas and is a realization that we are not separate from each other. We are all completely connected, embedded in one creation. As we get to further jhānas, this sub-tle awareness becomes a definite experience. Such unity-consciousness facil-itates loving-kindness and compassion because there is no separation between "me" and others. There is simply a quality of the heart, nothing else.

Once the mind is able to elevate itself, lift itself out of its ordinary way of thinking that is concerned with analysis, logic, and understanding, often very negative, then it also elevates all other mind-states we have. Our environment is dependent on us. It is a great mistake to think, as practi-cally the whole of humanity does, "There is the environment, and here I am. I can manipulate all I encounter for my own advantage." This is a completely wrong view. There is no boundary between us and our environ-ment, which is both other people and the whole of the natural world. We are all dependent on each other. So if we want a less-polluted environment, it will depend on a less-polluted mind, one that has the ability to reach higher states of consciousness. These states are not confined to the jhānas, but are dependent upon them.

6

# The Fourth Meditative Absorption

Although the absorptions that follow may not yet be a part of our practice, I think it is important to know what the meditative mind can do and where it can lead us. Even if we have only taken the first few steps, we need to see the whole road map. Then we return to the point we have reached personally and continue on our journey.

> Again, with the abandonment of pleasure and pain, and with the disappearance of previous joy and grief, he reaches and remains in the fourth jhāna, a state beyond pleasure and pain, purified by equanimity and mindfulness.

This does not mean that we have had pain or grief in the previous jhānas, though sometimes it is misunderstood in this way. Rather, it means that at this time all the emotions, both pleasurable and painful, are left behind. We reach a state of equanimity and mindfulness. For the word "mindfulness" we can always substitute "one-pointedness," which is a clearer description of what actually happens during the meditative absorptions. "Equanimity" is, in fact, the result of having been in the fourth jhāna. The experience is one of stillness, and at that time the mind cannot and should not say "this is equanimity," because that of course would take us out of the stillness.

I like to compare the third and fourth jhānas with a well. When we are in the third, it is as if we were sitting on the edge of the well, and letting ourselves down into it just a little, where it is much quieter than on the rim. To experience the fourth jhāna, we have to go right down to the bottom of the well. Obviously, we are going to reach various stages of stillness on our way down. It could also be compared to being completely covered by the ocean, but the well gives perhaps a better picture of the deepening that happens. In the third jhāna there is already peacefulness, but we can hear sounds, though we will not be disturbed by them, unless they are very loud. Then, as we deepen our concentration, sounds disappear because the mind is totally focused on the stillness and experiences nothing else.

This is something we will never encounter outside of meditation, though there will, of course, have been moments of peacefulness and contentment in our lives. But the world attacks us through our senses. We see, hear, taste, touch, smell, and think. Even though we may believe we are simply hearing or simply seeing, in fact, the mind has to digest what is seen and heard. Utter stillness is unknown to us. For if we really want to have complete stillness, complete peacefulness, the observer has to merge temporarily with the observed. There is no other way of getting into the fourth jhāna.

In the first three jhānas the observer can, to some extent, be standing apart from the experience. In the fourth this is not possible. The observer becomes so diminished that afterward we have the impression that no personal identity has been present. That is why the best description of the experience, the only possible one, is being submerged in "stillness." In actual fact, the observer has not really disappeared, for that happens only at what is called a "path-moment," which will be described later. To say that the observer has merged with the observed means that our self-assertion and ego support system have, for the duration of the meditation, been discarded. This is the reason why many people are afraid to go so deep into meditation. Their ego, their feeling of "me," is against it. To let go of that self, even temporarily, even though not completely, can be too frightening for the untrained mind. Instead of letting ourselves fall into this stillness, we back out. This is not uncommon. But it does not matter, we can always try again. It is like being afraid of the deep end of the swimming pool, when we are not quite sure we can really swim. But once we have had the experience of complete stillness and understood that it only comes through the temporary abandonment of our self-assertion, our will to be, and our desire for any kind of position, we realize how wonderful that abandoning of "self" actually is. Then we become ever more eagerly inclined to abandon it completely.

The fourth jhāna brings greatly increased mental energy. Most of us overwork our minds. We think all day and we dream all night. The mind is the most valuable tool in the whole universe; there is nothing comparable to it, yet we do not give it a moment's rest. The only time it can be at rest is when it stops thinking, reacting, emoting, and noting. Then it can just "be" in its original purity. The mind has glimpses of this in the first three jhānas, but it is only in the fourth that it actually experiences no disturbance at all. The regular practice of the fourth jhāna brings greater purification and therefore more clarification, so that the mind becomes more powerful.

Powerful minds are rare. Most minds move in accustomed ways; on hearing something, or reading something, our thoughts follow a familiar pattern. When we have been educated to think in a particular way, that is the pattern our minds will follow. It is highly unusual to have the ability to think in an independent manner and have the strength of mind to cut through all extraneous matter. The fourth jhāna makes this possible through the increased energy it gives to the mind.

When we misuse the body, going without sleep, not allowing it enough rest, what happens? We grow so weak that after only a few days we become incapable of functioning at all. But when it comes to the mind, although it never has any rest, we still believe we are quite capable of functioning at top capacity. The Buddha called the untrained mind "being asleep while awake." This means not understanding what we experience. We are all confronted with impermanence and dukkha, and should we search for an experiencer, none of us could find one. Yet we do not know these truths. We have the experience without the recognition.

When we come out of the fourth jhāna, we should feel rejuvenated in the mind. It is strength of mind that is addressed here. On the one hand, we gain the strength that comes through resting the mind, and on the other hand, we gain insight into the loss of ego-assertion, which brings about complete and utter stillness, where nothing at all happens. The mind has finally been allowed a holiday and a return to its original state of purity.

The holidays we usually take are quite exhausting, are they not? This one is really peaceful. We get a taste of letting go of all our ego supports, which means that we recognize the mistaken view that there is an ego. Because we now have an inkling of the final goal, our commitment to the path is likely to grow far stronger.

The experience of the fourth jhāna provides easier access to equanimity. Equanimity, one of the seven factors of enlightenment, is the highest emotion there is. We can experience it on several levels. The first is when we no longer become agitated should something happen that we do not like. This can be because we think it is not "the done thing" and we do not like to feel or look foolish; it can be because we are suppressing our reactions, or it can be because we have actually realized that, in the long run, whatever may be happening, is of no consequence. All things inevitably fall apart, anyway. Then there is equanimity as an emotional state which we arouse when necessary.

The Buddha talked about the five noble powers, the *ariyā iddhis*. *Ariyā* is "noble," and *iddhi* is "power" (Sanskrit, *siddhi*). The siddhis are very often described as magical powers, such as the ability to move the body instantaneously from one place to another, and the Buddha was once asked whether it was important to possess such powers. He answered by saying, "I will tell you about the five noble powers." He often altered the whole context of the question by changing the meaning of a word. He then went on to describe these powers. The first is that whenever we become aware of something unpleasant, we should immediately look for whatever is pleasant in it, not giving ourselves the chance to react negatively. By looking at its pleasant features, we arouse equanimity. The second is, when we become aware of something pleasant, we should immediately look at its unpleasant features, and through this, too, we arouse equanimity and do not become immersed in desire. The unpleasant feature of anything pleasant is its impermanence. We need to bear this in mind. Most people think they are quite aware of impermanence, quite accepting of it, but in fact they would much rather forget it, and constantly do so. But we should always remember that everything with which we come into contact is impermanent. Every single moment of our lives, pleasant or unpleasant, is one moment in eternity. In order to counteract greed, or desiring what is pleasurable, we recognize the impermanence of that pleasure. Conversely, we recognize that there are lovable features even in something very unpleasant. For example, if it is a person, we recognize that they also have dukkha, and therefore need our compassion. Furthermore, that they are also looking for happiness and therefore might need help. If it is a difficult situation, then the pleasant side to it is its inherent learning situation. Instead of becoming irate and negative, we see it in this positive light. This brings us the equanimity we need, at the required time.

The next two noble powers are quite similar: to remember both sides in the pleasant and also in the unpleasant. The fifth noble power, which applies only to an Arahant, an Enlightened Being, is to be aware of both aspects instantly, without effort, thereby without creating greed or hate. In the Buddha's day, nothing was written down; consequently, his teaching was often given in this somewhat repetitive form, so that it would be easier to commit to memory.

For us that means arousing equanimity in spite of our tendencies toward greed and hate, which entails remembering that such is the path of purification. This is the second kind of equanimity.

The third kind of equanimity does not leave us ever again, because we have become so imbued with the awareness of impermanence that we have it, so to speak, constantly at our fingertips. Our ego assertion has been reduced to the point where it is no longer an obstacle to equanimity. Whatever happens, needs to happen, and that is all. If it is exactly what we wanted, that is fine, and if it is not, that is fine too. That kind of equanimity is based on insight and is reinforced in the fourth jhāna.

Our insights need to be grounded in an imperturbable mind. Without calm in the mind, there can be no insight. Our ability to experience total stillness in the fourth jhāna is the essential foundation. From it comes the insight that this stillness, or equanimity, is only possible when we are without ego assertion. Once we realize this, we can experience equanimity whenever we wish, and we do not have to work so hard at it.

It is worth mentioning here that while the far enemy of equanimity is obviously excitement, restlessness, and anxiety, the near enemy is indifference. Indifference is often a protection against emotion. People who have had unhappy experiences, who have been hurt, whose feelings have run away with them, often try to protect themselves from their own negative emotions. But in attempting never to be upset, angry, or full of hate, they actually push down all other emotions too. The result is indifference. Having built a wall around themselves, they no longer have access to their feelings of loving-kindness and compassion. They do not want to get involved, perhaps because in the past they found that involvement led to unpleasant interactions. But this attitude closes the heart. We can sometimes become aware of this in the sweeping method of meditation referred to earlier. If we experience little or no sensation in the chest area, we may find that there is some kind of blockage present. It may feel like a brick or cement wall, or anything that seems unusually hard. This is the armor we have put on to protect ourselves from unwanted emotions and reactions. Indifference is called the near enemy of equanimity because it can appear very similar and it may be difficult to distinguish between them. We may believe that we are above all excitement and agitation, only to find that the loving aspect of ourselves is undeveloped. There is all the difference in the world between equanimity, which comes through insight, and indifference, which is really self-protection. Equanimity born of insight puts no blocks on loving-kindness and compassion. On the contrary, they both flow more easily because there is no wanting of anything in return, no expectation of a result. It is well worth our while to investigate this further and to discover whether we do in fact have any problem with indifference.

> His former true but subtle sense of equanimity and happiness vanishes, and there arises a true but subtle sense of neither happiness nor unhappiness, and he becomes one who is conscious of this true but subtle sense of neither happiness nor unhappiness.

What is being described here is "no emotion"—no happiness, no unhappiness. Even the contentment and peacefulness of the third jhāna have to be dropped, in order to get into the state where there is really only stillness. We are then beyond pleasure and pain, purified by equanimity and mindfulness. This purification has to take place before we can actually experience utter stillness. Our mindfulness and one-pointedness have to be absolute at this time. There can be no wavering. In the first three jhānas the mind may still move slightly, but not in the fourth. Equanimity must be present too, so that we are able to let go of all the pleasures of the first three absorptions. Delightful sensations, joy, contentment, and peacefulness are all relinquished in order to get to absolute stillness.

The "true but subtle sense of neither happiness nor unhappiness" is subtle because it is not something we recognize clearly enough at the time to actually say: "Now I am neither happy nor unhappy." What we experience is stillness. Afterward, when we come out of the jhāna and ask ourselves "What did I learn from this?" we may realize that we were neither happy nor unhappy, and therefore must have been in a balanced state of equanimity. But usually this is not verbalized in this way. We say "stillness without any noticeable observer" and realize what that means for us. The Buddha gives a simile for the fourth jhāna:

> Just as if a man were to sit wrapped from head to foot in a white garment, so that no part of him was untouched by that garment—so his body is suffused…[with that mental purity and clarification, so that no part of his body is untouched by it].

Here again we must not get a wrong impression of the word "body." Once we have actually been in the fourth jhāna, we will know what is meant. It is not really a physical sensation; it is an overall experience. It is impossible for the body itself to feel equanimity and mindfulness, or clarity and purification. The mind feels all that. We do, however, feel completely drowned in the stillness. It would be clearer and easier to understand if we were to substitute the word "being" for "body."

> And so, with a mind concentrated, purified and cleansed, unblemished, free from impurities, malleable, workable, established, and having gained imperturbability, he directs and inclines his mind towards knowing and seeing.

All these qualities of the mind are the result of the jhānas. We do not actually experience these states while the mind is totally quiet and still, but we can recognize these changes within ourselves when we inquire into our mind-states. In other discourses, the Buddha says that one can "direct the mind to knowing and seeing" after the third jhāna too. One can certainly do so after the fourth, fifth, sixth, and seventh jhānas, which are particularly useful for that. "Knowing and seeing" means to have the knowledge and vision of things as they really are, which is the understood experience. Vision does not mean picturing; rather, it is the ability to internalize the teaching while "knowing" is understanding what is seen.

After any of the jhānas, but more profoundly starting from the third one, the mind is able and willing to recognize a different reality, which at other times it cannot see. The reality is that there is no personal identity to be found. This is often challenged by questions such as: "If that is so, then who is meditating?" or "Then who is being perturbed?" These questions mean that the mind is revolting at the possibility that we are operating under an illusion, which actually brings us untold miseries. It is trying to revert to its usual stance: "Since I am here, it must be me." That is at the level of relative reality and relative truth. It does not bring liberation or freedom. We can help ourselves psychologically at this level if we purify thought-content and emotion, and we should certainly do this. But liberation—to be free, to be totally at ease, just to be there and nothing else—is only possible if we first understand the final goal of the Buddha's teaching and then draw nearer to it.

As we can see from the passage quoted above, in order to draw nearer to the knowledge and vision of the understood experience, we have to become calm. There is no possible way that a mind that is still rummaging about in the world can see the absolute reality of the truth that there is only mind and body and nothing else. We may be able to agree to it intellectually if we have read or heard enough of the Buddha's teaching, if we have been, so to speak, brainwashed enough. "Oh yes," we might say, "*anattā* means there is no one there." But truly to feel it within, with a mind that during meditation is still concerned with all the things that happen through the senses, simply cannot be done. On the contrary, we actually experience the opposite of the reality we want to fathom.

The truth we can and will find though is an underlying purity of mind, totally without any pull toward "having," or push toward "getting away from." It is clear, translucent, part of creation, part of universal consciousness, does not have any individuality, and does not make any demands. How can we recognize that reality when our senses are engaged; when we have to react to them simply in order to interpret what is going on in the world? We may neither like nor dislike, but we still have to know. But here, with a mind that is totally imperturbable, we have the chance to recognize a different, inner experience.

How do we begin to understand anattā? The Buddha continues:

And he knows: "This my body is material, made up from the four great elements, born of mother and father, fed on rice and gruel, impermanent, liable to be injured and abraded, broken and destroyed, and this is my consciousness which is bound to it and dependent on it."

So in the first instance, we look at the body and at the four elements of which it is composed—earth, fire, water, and air. The earth element is characterized by solidity and its function is supportive. The fire element consists of temperature and acts as destroyer, also rejuvenator. Water means all liquidity and is the binding element. Air or wind are life-infusing and function as movement. We can easily see that our bodies incorporate these four great elements and nothing more.

"Born of mother and father, fed on rice and gruel" are cause and effect. There is a cause for this body; we ourselves are causing it to be here; we are eating in order to maintain it. It arose at our birth, which was caused by our craving to exist. Without that craving, there would be no birth. It does not just happen by pure chance. There is no chaos in the universe; on the contrary, it is all quite orderly, subject to the laws of nature.

We want to take a look at the body and recognize that it is not "me." How do we do that? It certainly looks like me, does it not? We only have to look in the mirror to know, "Yes, that is me." But there are many ways in which we can get at the understanding that it is only a body. First of all, we can see that it is totally impermanent. It changes all the time. For one thing, it gets older. Most people will take that in their stride, simply accepting that they do not look as good as they once did. But what about the breath? If we tried to make that permanent, by holding it, what would happen? We would choke and possibly die. Breath is never permanent. Then too, when we have established mindfulness to the point where we have become deeply aware of our own body, in a way that is more meaningful than just knowing its movements, we can feel a constant pulsation. All the cells in our body are continually falling apart and coming together again. Science tells us that in a cycle of seven years, every single cell we have will die and be renewed. What else? We put food and drink into the body, and what happens? We have to digest, use them up, and excrete. In and out. Nothing remains permanently. What we ate a week ago is gone; we must always nourish ourselves afresh.

As long as we believe, "this is my body, this is me," our desires will never lessen because most of these desires are bound up with our bodies.

It is worth our while to check this out and see if it is so.

We have this wonderful notion that the body can be made perfect. The Buddha however said that the body did not get cancer; it was a cancer. Take a look at all the things that have to come out of the body in order to keep us healthy. None of them are very appealing. I am sure we would be reluctant to put them back in again. See the body for what it is; a necessary part of being a human being. Much of our dukkha comes through the body; we get "hung up" on it at many levels, always trying to satisfy the cravings associated with its demands. We can remember that the body is made up of the four elements and look at the four elements in ourselves. We can feel the solidity and compactness of our body and then stand next to a tree and touch its solid trunk. When we stand on the grass, we feel the dew and the juice of the grass and are aware of our own saliva, tears, perspiration, and pulsating blood. We feel the warmth of our own body and the warmth of the earth around us. We become aware of the wind on our face and our own breath. We see the wind moving clouds and leaves and relate that to our own movements. We can see there is no difference in materiality, in being; it just is. Our bodies are material, as the Buddha says, and the four elements are the foundation for all existence.

It is important to recognize the unsatisfactoriness of the body. This does not mean rejecting it, denying it, or thinking "it would be better if I didn't have a body at all." We simply understand that it creates problems for us. Then, through our realization of its impermanence, we are able to recognize our own mortality—not theoretically, or with the hope that it will not happen yet; not as a future event, but rather as a moment-to-moment happening. We are dying in the here and now. All our thoughts, all our emotions, our breath, our whole body, are constantly in flux. This continual movement is in us, just as it is in the whole universe, a moment-to-moment death and rebirth. Understanding this truth, we can also understand the larger-scale rebirth that occurs every morning when we wake from sleep. There is no need for us to speculate about what happens after we die. It is happening now, at each instant. As the body ages, this rebirth becomes more and more frail and fragile, until finally it does not happen any more. Mortality is now.

Can any of us remember what we thought yesterday at four-thirty in the afternoon? It is impossible. We have no inkling of it. Never mind what happened in our last birth, we cannot even recall what happened in this one. We can remember important or exciting events or situations, but they are few and far between. All the rest is past history, over and done with, and now totally forgotten.

The body is "impermanent, liable to be injured and abraded, broken and destroyed." We know how easy it is to fall ill or meet with an accident. It is not at all difficult to destroy a body; it is being done all the time, in wars, in lethal arguments, in accidents.

As we consider the Buddha's words, we need to investigate whether the body really is owned by anyone or whether it is, in fact, an impersonal creation, born out of the craving for existence, made up of the four elements, maintained by the food it eats, impermanent, and easily destroyed. Once we are able to see that it is all cause and effect, that the body has no "personality" as such, we will recognize the fact that we have little jurisdiction over it. Nobody wants to fall ill, have an aching back, a cold, or a headache, but we are all subject to such things. What does this mean? If we really owned the body and were in charge, how could these things happen? Another misconception is that if we purify our minds, our bodies will never give us trouble. That is one of the "New Age" wonders, very much in vogue today. The Buddha himself fell ill and died. We need to remember that everyone who ever lived has died. Everyone who is here now will die. If it were true that overcoming death and disease lies in our power, why has no one ever been able to do it? It is not borne out by facts, and it is not borne out by spiritual teachings. Of course we should look after our bodies, just as we look after the houses we live in. But none of us would consider our house to be ourselves, or be under the illusion that it would last forever, or would need no repair however well we maintained it. None of us would dream of thinking that way. This body is the house we live in, and we should keep it clean and orderly, do our best for it, but that is all. We can never make it perfect. By far the most important thing we can do is to look at it and ask ourselves: "Who owns it? What are its functions? Why does it do so many things I do not want it to do?"

"This is my consciousness, which is bound to it, and dependent on it." This is the very first step of insight—that there are body and mind, or consciousness, as it is called here. Yet another current New Age idea is that the two are totally and intrinsically one. Not only is that impossible, but it would not in fact be very pleasant, for if mind and body were one, we would never be able to develop equanimity toward our body's aches and pains. This kind of teaching, or viewpoint, is well intentioned, but where it contradicts the actual facts, it is not helpful. There is, however, a "unity consciousness," where we feel at one with all other creatures, with all nature, where we see no difference between "me" and everything that exists, and it occurs because we have let go of the dominating, overriding idea of personality.

Mind and body are two different phenomena, but dependent on each other. This dependence arises because we live in the human realm. The body, so to speak, carries the mind around. We do not have freedom from the body, though there are other realms—and we will hear of them later— where it is not necessary to have this kind of a body. Unfortunately for us, our mind is dependent on the body. If we have very painful sensations, the mind becomes irate, negative, disliking, or rejecting. If the sensations are pleasant, it becomes grasping and clinging. The mind reacts to what the body feels. That, however, is not necessarily a permanent situation. The Buddha used to say that the unenlightened person is troubled by two things, body and mind, whereas the enlightened person is troubled by only one, the body, for the mind no longer has to react. There is this possibility of independence from bodily sensations, but for us, in our unenlightened state, there is still interdependence between the two.

When we look at the four elements of the body, we see its configuration. In the same way, we can look at the mind and see its four aspects as well. In doing this, we will come nearer to the understanding that in fact there is nobody who owns it. The first aspect is "sense-consciousness," the five senses: seeing, hearing, tasting, touching, and smelling. The second aspect is feeling, which arises from sense-contact. This feeling is either pleasant, unpleasant, or neutral. The third is perception, which can also be called labeling. For example, when the feeling is unpleasant, the label is "pain." The fourth is mental formation, or reaction. If the mind has said "pain," the reaction is usually "I don't like it," or "I've got to get away from this." It is very useful at this stage in our practice to become clearly aware of these four aspects of mind and of how they follow each other as cause and effect: sense-contact, feeling, perception, and lastly, reaction. It is important to get to know this sequence, both during meditation and in our everyday life. The Buddha taught that it is through an awareness of these four parts of mind, through the knowledge and vision of the understood experience, that we come to the realization that there is nothing at all within them that constitutes a "me." The "me" is a thought, an idea. It is so deeply ingrained that we believe it wholeheartedly, and we find everyone around us believing it too.

This "me," however, is not only an idea, it is also the mechanism that produces greed and hate. We all know these two; they come very easily to us. We all live with them and are familiar with them, but they do not produce happiness. In our practice we need to examine not only the four elements as we experience them in the body, but also the four parts of mind and how they arise and cease. We can become aware of each sense-contact—a taste, a smell—and how such contact leads to the next step, feeling—pleasant, unpleasant, neutral—and so on.

Most people are only aware of the first and the last step, the sense-contact and the reaction: "It looks nice, I want it," or "It looks awful, I must get rid of it." The reaction follows so quickly that we miss out completely on the two intervening stages. We should practice in the following way: Having noticed our reaction, we go back to the sense-contact that led to it. We then try to become aware again of the feeling that followed the sense-contact, and then of the mind's explanation, its labeling (dirty, disgusting, delicious, boring). Notice these two missing parts, the feeling and the label. Now, within those four parts—sense-contact, feeling, perception, reaction—try to find the one who senses, feels, perceives, reacts. The mind says, "But it's me doing that," but this is only an idea. Where is this doer? We can actually notice that these four steps are an automatic progression, that there is no one "doing" anything. It all just happens and we can watch it happen.

We can also decide to stop the sequence at any of the four points, particularly at the perception, the labeling. Then we will notice that we are not compelled to react. As we do this, however, the mind will say: "Surely I must be the one who made that decision, who determined to do that." You can now try to find that one. There is only determination, which is a mental factor. It is essential to investigate this not once, but many times. Within these *khandhas*, these aggregates, lies the illusion. One person will say the determination came from their thinking, another that it came from their feeling, someone else will say: "It was the observer" or "It was my willpower." Then we need to ask ourselves if any of these can really be called "me"? Where is that "me" when none of these reactions are taking place, when there is no observer, no willpower, nothing like that going on at all? When any one of these supposed "me's" is not functioning, where is it? What is it doing? This needs good concentration and a great willingness to really find absolute truth, to get to the bottom of human existence and not simply to stay at the superficial level where we live with our likes and dislikes. If we have liked and disliked long enough, we may be able at this point to see that there must be another solution.

It is useful to do this investigation after a concentrated meditation. Otherwise it is likely to stay at the level of an intellectual exercise, and the mind may be quite happy to agree, simply because it wants to get away from all this enquiring. It wants it to stop, so it says "Yes, yes, of course. That's fine." If we investigate at this superficial level it brings no benefit whatsoever, but when that investigation leads to a realization, the benefit is great. It is an "Ah ha" experience. We must be careful, however, not to fall into the trap of thinking that it is "me" who is saying "Ah ha." It is the mind that says that!

The Buddha gives a simile for the insight that comes from the experience of the fourth jhāna:

> It is just as if there were a gem, a beryl, pure, excellent, well cut into eight facets, clear, bright, unflawed, perfect in every respect, strung on a blue, yellow, red, white or orange cord. A man with good eyesight, taking it in his hand and inspecting it, would describe it as such. In the same way, a monk with mind concentrated, purified and cleansed,... directs his mind towards knowing and seeing. And he knows: "This my body is material, made up of the four great elements,... and this is my consciousness which is bound to it and dependent on it."

A gem, perfect in every respect, is the image of the insight, which is clear, bright and unflawed. Just as the recognition of the gem requires good eyesight, so insight needs a pure and concentrated mind.

There has to be a relationship between what is being seen, or investigated, and our inner being. It is the mind that does the investigation:

"Who is having the sense-contact? Who is reacting?" But as we investigate, there must also be a connection to our inner feeling, which may assert over and over again, "This is me." When we feel that, we simply investigate further. Though it is quite accurate that this is indeed what is being felt, it does not hold water when we investigate it at length and in detail. It is only a mistaken view. We continue to look at the great elements, the causes for the arising of the body, its impermanence, our own mortality, any of these, or all of them, if we really want to know. We also investigate the four parts of mind as they successively arise. "Who is doing all this, and very often against my will? Why is it happening when I would much rather be in the fourth jhāna?"

In this way, we can get nearer to an understanding of what the Buddha really taught. If we just stay on the surface, we will never be able to use his road map correctly. His promise was that if we go the whole way, there would be no more dukkha ever again. If through our practice we gain confidence in what he says, we may want to follow his map in every detail and continue on our journey.

# 7

# The Fifth and Sixth Meditative Absorptions

## *"Infinity of Space, Infinity of Consciousness"*

There are some apt similes for the first four meditative absorptions given by Buddhaghosa in his commentary, the *Visuddhimagga*, written in the fifth century.[3]

A man is wandering through the desert, carrying no water with him, and growing thirstier and thirstier. At last, he sees a pool in the distance and is filled with excitement and delight.

To wander through the desert feeling very thirsty represents our inner yearning for joy, happiness, and peace, which we try unsuccessfully to satisfy in the outside world. The excitement and delight experienced on seeing the pool in the distance correspond to the feeling that arises in the first jhāna—the realization that there is something that, though it is still "in the distance," can ultimately bring us complete satisfaction. Knowing it is there, the mind moves toward it.

Next, the man stands at the edge of the pool and is extremely joyful, knowing he has reached the water that will take away his thirst. This describes the second jhāna, the joy of knowing that we have come to the brink of inner satisfaction.

He then climbs into the pool and drinks, and having drunk all he needs, he feels contented and quite a different person from the one who was wandering around in the desert without any water.

This is the experience of the third jhāna. If we have ever been without water for a long period, we know how distressing that would be, both physically and mentally. The simile refers to our normal mental and emotional states, for while we are searching, we are always agitated and ill at ease, but once we have "drunk what we need," the difference is enormous. We experience joy and contentment. This delightful state is not the final goal of the Buddha's teaching, but only a step on the way. It is, however, a vital step, for it gives us the impetus to carry on and also to gain new insights.

Now the wanderer in the desert feels at peace. Earlier, restlessly searching, he was in a very unpleasant situation, for water is an absolute necessity for physical survival. His need pushed him in all directions. Now that he has slaked his thirst, he climbs out of the pool, goes to a shady tree, and lies down to recover from his great exertions. This feeling of being totally at ease is experienced in the fourth jhāna. Not that we fall asleep, but rather that, in the stillness of the jhāna, the mind comes to rest.

These similes describe very well what we go through in life, sometimes without even knowing what is happening. Just as we cannot live without water, so are joy and peace essential for our inner fulfillment. We may not even be aware that we are searching for something. It manifests only in our restlessness as we move from here to there, trying out different friends, different ideas, different jobs, different countries. Whatever we attempt is a reflection of our inner thirst, which we hope to quench in all these external ways. What we are looking for lies within us, and if we gave our time and energy to an interior search, we would come across it much faster, since that is the only place where it is to be found.

It is said that the fourth jhāna is the springboard for the formless jhānas that follow. We are all capable of reaching these states of consciousness; in fact, they might almost be called "nothing special." They are certainly not enlightenment, but they are the foundation and implementation of our mind-capacity. Enlightenment itself is something special and requires a great deal of mental strength, so we must first lay the foundations. The meditative absorptions are only a matter of patience and perseverance, while, above all, not looking for any achievement or result.

The first four jhānas are called the "fine-material absorptions" because we have similar states in ordinary life, though far less fulfilling and always dependent on outer conditions. We can, however, relate to these jhānas fairly easily because of that. All these absorption states are already within us, and all that obscures them from our view are our own thought processes. Whatever the thought might be, whether "I have to concentrate," or "I must do this," or "I don't want to do that," is of no consequence. The absorptions are hidden from us by our thinking, emoting, reacting, opinions, and viewpoints—all things with which we are utterly familiar. When we realize that we have never been completely satisfied by our usual activities of mind and body, then there is only one answer: to let them go during meditation and not allow them to enter the mind. Whether "I" like something or do not like it, whether "I" want to achieve something or not, makes no difference and has no bearing on our meditation. When we let the whole conglomeration drop, the mind automatically reverts to other states of consciousness. This is what the Buddha is explaining to Poṭṭhapāda. We all have consciousness, and therefore we are also capable of accessing those states of awareness known as the meditative absorptions.

People have written and spoken in conflicting ways about the absorptions, giving rise to a great deal of confusion. It is easier if we have not been exposed to any of this because then there are no preconceived ideas that may hamper us, and we can simply sit down and do it. If we drop whatever may be going on in the mind, the rest happens quite naturally, because this is where the calm and collected mind goes. It has nowhere else to go until it has reached Nibbāna, and then it can move into the bliss of Nibbāna. Until then, these are the only states it can experience, once it has dropped everything else. It is not even necessary to "get" concentrated. All we have to do is let go of our thought processes. Just as a dog jumps into a pool, comes out, and rids itself of all the water that has collected on its coat, we shake it all off.

The next steps are known as the formless meditative absorptions. In Pali, the first four are called the *rūpa* jhānas, and the next four, the *arūpa* jhānas. *Rūpa* means "form." *A* means "non," or "not." These jhānas are known as formless because, when we are using our mental abilities in an ordinary, everyday way, we have no connection to them. In fact, to a non-meditator, they could sound like a fairy tale. A meditator, even without having experienced them, might have a glimmer of understanding. As we saw in the previous chapters, the first four jhānas concern physical sensations and emotions. The similes given by the Buddha all refer to the body: it should be suffused, drenched, or, in the fourth jhāna, completely covered. In these next jhānas, no such similes are given, and no emotions, and certainly no physical sensations are touched upon. These are strictly mental states, and they come about because the mind, through constant practice of the first four absorptions, has grown malleable, pliable, and flexible enough to experience them. It has lost its rigidity and resistance, and is now capable of reaching these next higher levels.

The Buddha describes the fifth jhāna thus:

> Again, by passing entirely beyond bodily sensations, by the disappearance of all sense of resistance and by non-attraction to the perception of diversity, seeing that space is infinite, he reaches and remains in the Sphere of Infinite Space. In this way, some perceptions arise through training, and some pass away through training.

In the fourth jhāna we no longer experience bodily sensations but are only aware of the stillness of our mind, our emotions, and feelings. So in the fifth jhāna, "passing entirely beyond bodily sensations" is not something that has to be done specifically. Rather, it is "all sense of resistance" that must be deliberately dropped. This refers, first and foremost, to the limitation of the body as we normally experience it. We conceptualize a distinct boundary: "Where my skin ends is where my body ends," and that is where "I" end too, or so we believe. There is a definite resistance, a limit we impose on ourselves. In the first four fine-material absorptions, that boundary has already been enlarged to some extent. At any rate, it is not quite as rigid and restricted as it is in our ordinary everyday life, where we know exactly where we begin and end, or at least imagine we do; we see ourselves as filling a prescribed space.

When we come out of fourth jhāna and want to reach "the infinity of space," we can notice the boundaries of the body, wherever they may be at the moment, and start stretching its limits further and further. The contemplation on the four elements, referred to earlier, gives some inkling of this process.

The Buddha speaks of "non-attraction to the perception of diversity." We need to get beyond that attraction to "singleness" of one person, one house, one tree, one forest, one sky, one horizon. We perceive everything as separate, as having a boundary. This attraction to diversity is the natural human state. The Pali word for diversity is *papañca*, "manifoldness," and nature abounds in it. Within every species there are countless "individuals." Human beings are a case in point: we all look a little different from each other. We are attracted to that diversity. When we are in a forest, we enjoy the shape of each particular tree, the characteristics of each branch or leaf; we find that beautiful. Similarly, we look up at the sky and appreciate the single stars, or the moon. We do the same with people: attracted by one face, finding it pleasing, or turning away from another. We must go beyond all that in order to get into the infinity of space.

There are two methods of doing this, and we can use either or both depending on how difficult we find it to expand the mind sufficiently. One way, as mentioned above, is to go to the boundaries of the body, wherever they are experienced, and begin to expand them until they are totally dissolved in infinity. Should we come to a blockage where expansion seems to go no further, we can then use the perception of forests, meadows, mountains, valleys, rivers, oceans; then further to this whole globe we live on; and even further to the sky that surrounds it and the horizon. When we come to the horizon, we let go of that too, and there is the infinity of space. This is "non-attraction to diversity," or to the boundaries that, in our opinion, keep everything separate.

It is also helpful to reflect on these guidelines, asking ourselves whether there is truth in the Buddha's statement; is there, in fact, total unity, rather than the seeming diversity to which we are so attracted? Are the boundaries, which seem so real, nothing but an optical illusion? From a scientific point of view, it is common knowledge that there are no solid building blocks to be found anywhere in the universe. There are only particles of energy, endlessly coming together and falling apart. We have all heard of this but tend to forget it. If, through contemplation, we come to see that this really is the way things are, we will also recognize that our boundaries can only be mind-made illusion. This understanding will help us to let go of our attraction to diversity.

Above are two approaches to entering into the infinity of space, which, according to the Buddha's words, can be done quite deliberately. We do not have to wait for the great good fortune of perhaps one day chancing upon it. Being able to realize such an underlying truth helps to expand the mind. Most people never think in this way. They have no concept of total unity. Even scientists, who have come to this truth through experiment and investigation, rarely make it a part of their inner thought processes. They see it simply as a scientific fact. If, however, it is a truth, then it refers to our own mind, for mind is the underlying factor of the universe. This is not the personal, limited mind with which we are all familiar. If we give this realization some thought, we may find that we are able to reach that kind of mind extension. The less we limit the mind, the more it is able to expand, and the easier it is to see the highest truths. What we usually know has no bearing on absolute truth; it is narrowed down and distorted by our own limitations. If we expand the mind, we go beyond those limitations. We all have this potential, and in fact, as human beings, it is our responsibility to make the most of such potential; not to stay within our present limits, but to expand as far as we can go.

After any concentrated meditation, but particularly after any of the jhānas, it is most beneficial and worthwhile to direct the mind toward inquiry into "insight-wisdom."

In the following statement the Buddha deals with the mistaken views of the self, prevalent in his time. Because the language sounds archaic to our ears, we may jump to the conclusion that what is being said has no connection to the way we think today. On the contrary, it is exactly how we think.

> Certain ascetics and Brahmin declare and hold the view: since this self is material, composed of the four great elements, the product of mother and father, at the breaking-up of the body it is annihilated and perishes and does not exist after death. This is the way in which this self is annihilated.

The first thing we learn from this is that those who propounded this view—and Potthapāda was one of them—believed that the self is identical with the body, that this body is "me." This view is so widespread in our own age that it would be impossible to guess how many of us firmly believe it. From it comes the popular idea that if we perfect our bodies, we ourselves will be perfected. Firstly, we can never perfect the body, and secondly, even that would not make the essential difference. Physically, we may feel a little better, but that is all. This view, however, can be found today in almost any esoteric magazine.

We, of course, use a different type of language. We would not talk of being composed of four great elements, but the concept is exactly the same. We look in the mirror and say to ourselves "That is me." Who else could it be? We have looked so often in that mirror and always seen the same reflection. Of course it must be "me." This is a limited and limiting viewpoint. It cannot bring us fulfillment because the body itself can never be satisfied. It has needs that must constantly be met and demands that are sometimes quite absurd. The body brings us many problems. Think for a moment how it would be if we could sit on the meditation pillow with only a mind and no body. What a wonderful help to our meditation. We would never feel, "I can't endure this position a moment longer," never be troubled by painful knees, backache, an itch here, a sneeze there. Of course, we would still have to concentrate the mind, but we would be so much freer to do so. The body, to say the least, is a nuisance. Can we acknowledge that it is ridiculous to identify ourselves with it? Why should we think we are that nuisance? Yet, like Poṭṭhapāda and his acquaintances, we assume exactly that.

Next comes a second mistaken view of the self, one that sounds a little more grandiose:

> And another says: there is such a self as you say, I do not deny it. But that self is not wholly annihilated for there is another self, divine, material, belonging to the sense-sphere, fed on real food. You do not know it or see it, but I do. It is this self that at the breaking-up of the body perishes.

This is the identification with a soul. When the body breaks up, that particular person that we were is gone. But there is another divine self, which belongs to the "sense-sphere." A similar view is very widespread nowadays. We may not believe it intellectually, but it has been drummed into us for so long that we are left with an underlying doubt; perhaps there is a "me" in the soul, or a soul in me—whichever way we like to think of it—that will be quite different from the "me" we know now. The "soul-me" will be good. We do not like to admit that we have both sides in us, the wholesome and the unwholesome. We would like to think that the soul is our refined aspect, and that it will have the self in it. Even if we deny it intellectually, there is still this inner hope: "If I am not the body, at least I will be that." Another part of this belief system contains the notion that wherever the self goes after death, it will be happy.

The third view is:

> There is such a self as you say, I do not deny it. But that self
> is not wholly annihilated, for there is another self, divine,
> material, mind-made, complete with all its parts, not defective
> in any sense-organ. It is this self that at the breaking-up of the
> body perishes.

Here we have a subtle, mind-made idea that posits, not a soul, but a higher self. In Hinduism, this is the concept of union with Atman, the "absolute self," in contrast to a "particular self." The Buddha says that all this is quite wrong, which is why he is repeating these various mistaken viewpoints. The "mind-made self" is also a reference to the higher jhānas, the first of which is, as we have seen, "infinity of space." Experiencing such a state of consciousness brings about the idea that if "I" dissolve into that space, then that is the way the mind has made up the self.

All these concepts arise because people are unable to let go of the idea that there must be "someone" there. We continue to believe it. "Who is doing everything I'm doing?" we say to ourselves. "Who is thinking all the thoughts I'm thinking? Who is reacting to my sense-contacts? Who is wanting all the things I want? There has to be somebody there." Even if we no longer identify with the body, which is really not so difficult to do, we feel compelled to identify with something else. The first step would be the soul; the second would be a higher self, or through the formless absorptions, some kind of self that still exists within infinite space or infinite consciousness.

Lastly, a fourth wrong view is:

> There is such a self as you say, but there is another self which,
> by passing entirely beyond bodily sensations, by the disap-
> pearance of all sense of resistance, and by non-attraction to the
> perception of diversity, seeing that space is infinite, has real-
> ized the sphere of infinite space. It is this self that at the break-
> ing-up of the body perishes.

This is "self within unity." In the fifth jhāna, the ability to get into infinite space brings with it an experience of unity. We lose our separateness, our alienation. The idea of "unity-consciousness," popular at the moment, has a certain validity. It is the consciousness that we are not the observer, the one who stands apart and watches everything happening. As long as we are this observer we cannot help being judgmental, critical, disliking. We are beset with craving because we would like to get some of what we are observing, or we would like to get rid of some of it, but we are not embedded within all we experience. As long as we maintain this stance, we can believe in the body, or the soul, or the higher self. When we have the experience of unity, we may actually believe that we have discarded our ego-consciousness. This is the idea of union with God, or in Hinduism, with Atman. However, to unite, to join with something, implies that there is something or someone who can enter into such a union. Once again, the Buddha denies this viewpoint.

In each of these four wrong views there is still the idea, however subtle, of a "self." Certainly "unity-consciousness" is preferable to "separation-consciousness." It enables us to feel loving-kindness and compassion for others almost without effort, for if all is one, who can irk or irritate us? It also removes a lot of fear. When we feel alienated, we also feel threatened by others, by the world around us, and by death. When we feel at one with all that exists, whether we call it God, or Atman, or some other word, that fear is greatly diminished. The sense of self, however, is still present, for we still need it in order to unite with the higher ideal.

It is very much worth our while to contemplate these four views and ask ourselves to which of them we adhere. Is it identification with the body? The soul? The higher self? Is it union with creation? Who do we actually think we are? We may never have experienced unity-consciousness, but we can contemplate the idea and ask ourselves who or what unites. We can check out whether the soul is to be found within and whether that is "me." We can contemplate the higher self and the body. Is there really any foundation for seeing "me" in any one of these? Our convictions are deeply ingrained, and while the mind is still contracted, rather than malleable and expansive, it has great difficulty in seeing things as they are. It is very hard for us to grasp that these are all just belief systems invented by the mind in order to support the ego. When we no longer need or want to support this ego assertion, it becomes much easier to see a different reality. The clearer this reality becomes, the easier it is to meditate, for we begin to understand that the only thing that stands in the way of our practice is "me." The more clearly we grasp this "me" as simply an idea, the less will it obstruct our path.

The Buddha's teaching is not just a psychological aid to living. It is that too, but more importantly it is a radical re-thinking, followed by a radical re-experiencing. This is why it has endured for two thousand five hundred years. Psychology has its ups and downs, its fads and new ideas, but this teaching is so fundamental, nothing new can be added to it. As we practice, we try to see the whole gamut of experience that the Buddha has shown us. This is where our ability to contemplate and to investigate comes in. When we meditate, the mind is attempting to become calm and collected; when we contemplate, it is trying to see things in a different light. The two have to go hand in hand. There is a completeness, a unity, to the Buddha's teaching, as we can see from this sutta. We cannot just single out one part of it and practice that; it does not work that way. All must be included: moral conduct, guarding the senses, contentment, mindfulness, meditation or right concentration, contemplation, and investigation.

We now come to the sixth jhāna:

> Again, by passing entirely beyond the Sphere of Infinite Space, seeing that consciousness is infinite, he reaches and remains in the Sphere of Infinite Consciousness. In this way some perceptions arise through training, and some pass away through training.

These explanations of the formless absorptions are very brief, and we might suppose this is so because the Buddha realizes that Poṭṭhapāda is not ready yet for their actual practice, or that part of the explanation has been lost.

When, in the fifth jhāna, we experience the infinity of space, all we really have to do to get into the next jhāna is turn our attention from the spaciousness to the consciousness that has experienced it. Only infinite consciousness can experience infinite space. On emerging from the sixth jhāna, when we ask ourselves "What have I learned from this?" we realize that there is no such thing as personal identity, only unity. When we integrate this into our thought process, unity-consciousness arises. Neither in infinite space nor in infinite consciousness can we find a separate person who is experiencing a meditative absorption. Should we find one, then we are no longer concentrated on infinity, and the observer has resurfaced. In the fourth jhāna, the observer is minimal, which is a great aid to mental energy and clarity. In the fifth and sixth, the observer is more apparent, so when we come out of either one, the observer knows perfectly well that there was nobody and nothing except infinity, and can actually fully absorb that understanding.

With the experience of infinity of consciousness comes the realization that it is synonymous with universal consciousness. Once we have that understanding, in the form of actual experience, we will never want to soil universal consciousness with unwholesome thoughts, speech, or action. We are all, each one of us, part of it, and the more our own consciousness is purified, the easier it is for us to have access to the purity of universal consciousness. Within it, everything can be found. Whatever we think, say, or do is contained in it and does not disappear. This is another realization inherent in experiencing the jhānas.

We can compare the fifth and sixth jhānas with the first and second absorptions. When we have a delightful sensation, joy arises. All we have to do is shift our attention from the sensation to the emotion, which is already present and just needs our awareness. In the fifth and sixth jhāna, it is the same, only on a subtler level, for the absorptions become progressively finer tuned. With the experience of infinite space, the experience of infinite consciousness arises simultaneously. We simply turn our attention from the spaciousness itself to the consciousness that is aware of that.

Infinity of consciousness can be misunderstood. This was particularly so in the Hindu tradition, where it was often thought to be the epitome of spiritual attainment. The experience does give rise to an absolutely authentic realization, which is: "I am that," in Sanskrit *tat tvam asi*, describing unity-consciousness. Meister Eckhart, the medieval Christian mystic, worded it slightly differently when he said: "God and I are the same." He narrowly escaped being burned at the stake for this. He said it with no further explanation whatsoever, and I think we can assume that he reached the higher jhānic states. For otherwise it would be impossible to say such a thing, and say to it, as he did, not from pride but with humility, for his greatest endeavor was not to "be" anyone.

It is certainly a highly important realization and part of the meditative process. As, through practice, we develop this process and make it more and more our own, the level of clarity and understanding in the mind also rises simultaneously. It is no longer so limited and contracted that it can only be concerned with the "particular self." In meditation, it has reached something that is beyond even the "absolute self." However, though it may experience both infinite space and infinite consciousness, the mind will realize, when it comes out of these states of awareness, that dukkha is present again and that there is more to be done. As long as we feel a self within, that self will have dukkha. That is why it is important to investigate which "self" we believe in, and to ask ourselves whether there are any grounds for that belief. When we find it to be without foundation, we may experience quite a significant shift in our perception of how things really are.

# 8

# The Seventh *"The Sphere of No-thingness"*
# The Eighth *"Neither Perception nor Non-perception"*
# The Ninth Meditative Absorption *"Cessation"*

"Again, by passing entirely beyond the Sphere of Infinite Consciousness, seeing that there is no-thing, he reaches and remains in the Sphere of No-Thingness, and he becomes one who is conscious of this true but subtle perception of the Sphere of No-Thingness. In this way some perceptions arise through training, and some pass away through training. And this is that training," said the Lord.

This description of the seventh jhāna is just as brief as the preceding ones. The translator has inserted a hyphen into the word "nothingness," which is helpful. Otherwise we might misunderstand the term, or dismiss it, wondering how "nothingness" could ever be anything on which we could put our attention. Calling it "No-thingness" is clearer and more descriptive.

The fifth, sixth, and seventh jhānas are often known as the *vipassanā* or insight jhānas. Of course we also gain insights from the first four, as we have already seen. To recapitulate briefly: the first brings the insight that what we are looking for in the world is already within us; the second, that our sense-contacts can never provide us with the joy we experience in the jhāna itself; the third, that contentment and peacefulness can only arise where there is wishlessness. It is worth repeating here that wishing to get into any of these jhānas guarantees that they will not happen; we need to drop all wishes and simply relax into the experience. The fourth, that when ego assertion is minimized, stillness arises, and from that stillness comes even-mindedness, or equanimity.

The fifth and sixth jhānas bring the major insight that, during meditation, the person we think we are is not available. Space is there, consciousness is there, but although there is an observer, there is no person to be found. That observer has expanded to the infinity of space and consciousness, for otherwise neither could be known. The little observer who is sitting here now, reading these pages, trying to understand, cannot experience infinity. We do not look very infinite, do we? We do not feel very infinite either. But at the time of the jhāna, there is a feeling of infinity, and the observer is also infinite. Although there is space, which is materiality, and although there is consciousness, which is mind, there is nobody there who can claim to have either of these. They just are.

In the seventh jhāna, the Sphere of No-thingness, we realize that not only is there no person, there is no "thing." Neither in the infinity of space nor in the infinity of consciousness is there anything that can be grasped or held onto; not a single solid building block in the whole universe. To hear of such a truth, to read about it, is all very interesting, but to experience it for ourselves is another matter. Afterward, our reactions to the world and the people in it are bound to change, for we now possess the inner knowledge that, however solid everything and everyone may appear, in reality everything is in constant flux.

During the seventh jhāna itself, this can be experienced in two different ways. We may become aware of a constant, very subtle movement, as if we were looking at a fountain where the spray is constantly in motion; that is too gross a description, but it conveys some idea of it. The other possibility is that we become aware of a great expanse that combines infinity of space and the consciousness of it, and within that expanse there is no-thing to be found.

These profound insights cannot be assimilated straightaway; it takes time, and the jhānas must be repeated many times before the mind becomes imbued with this knowledge and vision. Then it becomes a gut feeling, and we can act upon it. It is not to be confused with Nibbāna, but it is certainly a taste of another dimension.

> Poṭṭhapāda, from the moment when a monk has gained this controlled perception, he proceeds from stage to stage till he reaches the limit of perception.

The term "controlled perception" refers to the jhānas, for it is during the jhānas that the mind first gains such control. Most people think they are already in control of their lives, which is just a lack of understanding. If that were really so, we would certainly never be so foolish as to allow ourselves to be unhappy. Control means that we can think what we choose to think and let go of all the things that are not conducive to our happiness and to the goal of our practice. The first time this happens is when the mind becomes one-pointed enough to experience the jhānas. Obviously, the higher the jhāna, the greater the degree of control, and it is with the third jhāna that controlled perception really begins. Then, as the Buddha says here, we proceed from stage to stage until we reach "the limit of perception."

This "limit of perception" is touched upon in the eighth jhāna, which provides the greatest restfulness for the meditating mind and thereby infuses us with the most energy possible. It is the final stage before "the extinction (cessation) of higher consciousness (perception)," sometimes known as the ninth jhāna, which is what Poṭṭhapāda was asking about in the first place. As we saw in chapter one, the Pali word for this is *abhisaññānirodha: abhi*, "higher"; *saññā*, "perception"; and *nirodha*, "cessation." It is usually referred to simply as *nirodha*. It is said in the scriptures that only nonreturners, or arahants, are able to enter into this jhāna.

In some of the writings and commentaries it is quite elaborately described. Such a person appears to be dead, for the breath has become so fine as to be unnoticeable. The life force has not, however, left the body, which retains a little heat and a very slow heartbeat. It is said that a meditator can remain in this "cessation" for up to seven days. It would not, however, be usual for a meditator to choose to do such a thing; it would be more commonly undertaken as some kind of display of mastery, of which the Buddha strongly disapproved.

> When he has reached the limit of perception it occurs to him: "Mental activity is worse for me, lack of mental activity is better."

What is meant here, and it is a very important insight, is that thinking itself is dukkha. Any wish, any desire, any activity in the mind is dukkha, because all thinking is forever moving. Movement is irritation, which creates dukkha, and can never be totally fulfilling. If we think about the past, for instance, we bring it into the present. If that past was unsatisfactory, we wish it had been different, thereby causing ourselves a lot of needless suffering. We should let the past rest. It is gone, there is no need to relive that unhappiness. We are alive now and practicing. The only thoughts that can benefit us are those that concern the path to liberation, as we experience it in the present moment. Equally, if we bring the future to mind, hoping for something we want, or praying that some other thing will not happen, we bring that also into the present and with it, dukkha. We need to look at ourselves honestly, though without judgment, and recognize how frequently we do this and how foolish it is.

To say "mental activity is worse for me, lack of mental activity is better" does not mean we should become unthinking vegetables! The Buddha himself had the sharpest of minds and was a genius at explaining the human situation. But, even outside of meditation, there are many moments in our day when there is no need to think. At these times we can simply be aware of what is: breath, movement, sight, hearing, with no explanations coming from the mind. We learn non-thinking through the jhānas, we practice it in everyday life, thereby giving the mind far more strength and energy, for we are not overworking it, as most of us habitually do.

"If I were to think and imagine, these perceptions that I have attained would cease, and coarser perceptions would arise in me. Suppose I were not to think or imagine?" So, the meditator realizes that these very subtle perceptions that arise in the seventh jhāna, and even more so in the eighth, cease as soon as we begin to think and imagine. Compared with the *jhanic* states, thinking, reacting, and projecting are all coarse perceptions. Projecting, particularly, is a very negative habit of mind. We project onto others what we carry within, but refuse to admit it to ourselves and then blame and dislike the other person. Of course, we have to live in the world, have a job, join in discussions; we have to go to that level of thought, there is no other way. The Buddha did so too. In this sutta he is talking to Poṭṭhapāda on a very ordinary mental level because he is answering questions and offering explanations. But there are both subtle and coarse perceptions, and the subtlety of our perceptions brings a finesse to our mind and to our whole being. We can truly say we are what we think, and we should take a cue from this, and always keep careful watch over our thought processes and what we choose to think about. The greater the care we take, the easier we will find the pathway and practice of the meditative absorptions.

> So he neither thinks nor imagines. And then, in him, just these perceptions arise, but other, coarser perceptions do not arise.

There are several ways of translating the verb "to imagine": "to manipulate, to plan, to perfect, to fancy"—all are possibilities. Since this is a dead language, spoken more than two thousand years ago, the task is not easy. But when we are neither thinking nor imagining, not planning, reacting, projecting, then the coarser perceptions do not arise. The duality of the world, what we like or do not like, what we think others should do or not do, none of that is present in the mind. The infinitely more subtle perceptions of the jhānas can only arise when we are able to let all that go. The Buddha continues:

> He attains cessation. And that, Poṭṭhapāda, is the way in which the cessation of perception is brought about by successive steps.

The eighth jhāna, which the Buddha does not elaborate on here, is known as "neither perception nor non-perception." It is "neither this nor that," a state of inactivity for the mind, in which observing has almost come to a complete halt. It is still present, but at such a refined level that we are neither perceiving, nor not-perceiving. Even at cessation, the ninth jhāna, there is still a very subtle perception of "me" for the nonreturner, which is likened to the aroma that clings to a flower. Only the arahant is entirely free from that. The Buddha now questions Poṭṭhapāda:

> "What do you think, Poṭṭhapāda? Have you heard of this before?"
> "No, Lord. As I understand it, the Lord has said: 'Poṭṭhapāda, from the moment when a monk has gained this controlled perception, he proceeds from stage to stage until he reaches the limit of perception.... He attains cessation... and

that is the way in which the cessation of perception is brought about by successive steps.'"

"That is right, Poṭṭhapāda."

So Poṭṭhapāda is a good student; he has listened and retained what he has been told. But now, having at last been given the answer to his original question, he immediately comes up with others:

Lord, do you teach that the summit of perception is just one, or that it is many?

The Buddha replies:

I teach it as both one and many.

And Poṭṭhapāda follows up with another question:

Lord, how is it one, and how is it many?

And the Buddha responds:

According as one attains successively to the cessation of each perception, so I teach the summit of that perception; thus I teach both one summit of perception, and I also teach many.

If we use the word "consciousness" rather than "perception," it may be easier for us to grasp what the Buddha is saying here. There is, in the first jhāna, a shift of consciousness. It is not yet very subtle, but it is, nonetheless, different. When we come out of the jhāna, that consciousness, the summit of our experience at that time, ceases. As we advance through the jhānas, it becomes progressively more subtle, each stage paving the way for the next, until we reach the last, "the summit of perception," which is the outer limit of human capability. Then follows cessation. The Buddha teaches both this final summit and also the stage-by-stage summits of each jhāna. Poṭṭhapāda is still not satisfied:

Lord, does perception arise before knowledge, or knowledge arise before perception, or do both arise simultaneously?

The Buddha answers:

Perception arises first, Poṭṭhapāda, then knowledge, and from the arising of perception comes the arising of knowledge. And one knows: "Thus conditioned, knowledge arises."

In chapter six we looked at the four aspects of mind: sense-consciousness, feeling, perception, and mental formation. So we already know that, in terms of cause and effect, perception has to arise before knowledge can follow. In other words, we have to have the experience before we can understand it. This holds true for everything we do. For instance, to understand the concept of impermanence, we first have to experience it in, say, the arising and ceasing of our breath or our thoughts. It is exactly the same, with the consciousness levels of the jhānas. They have to have taken place before we can "know" what has happened. The word "knowledge," as the Buddha uses it here, has been described in the early commentary to the Pali Canon, as "review-knowledge." This really comes to the same thing, for we can only review what has already happened. It is, in fact, the way to wisdom; for insight only arises through the understood experience. This is an important part of the Buddha's teaching. We all have the seed of enlightenment within, but because we do not truly understand our experiences, they bring us no insight and we remain unenlightened. The Buddha continues:

In this way you can see how perception arises first, and then knowledge, and that from the arising of perception comes the arising of knowledge.

At this stage, the Buddha is answering Poṭṭhapāda's questions directly, as he has already given him all the training steps. Poṭṭhapāda is obviously very interested in what is being said, but it is equally obvious that he is quite unfamiliar with any of it, for otherwise he would not be asking such questions. Now he comes up with another:

Lord, is perception a person's self, or is perception one thing, and self another?

This is a typical difficulty that arises when we look at things from the relative level of truth. We identify with the perception and call it "me." "Who else," we say, "could be observing what I am thinking? It must be me," and in this manner our thoughts go round and round in circles, and we never find a way out, because to do so, we would have to let go of all these ideas. It is the same with Poṭṭhapāda, who is totally immersed in the relative level of truth. We can easily identify with him, can we not? We can also have a great deal of compassion for him, for he is just like us.

The Buddha asks him, "Well, Poṭṭhapāda, do you postulate a self?" He is attempting to move Poṭṭhapāda away from the idea of a self but meets with no success, as we shall see.

Lord, I postulate a gross self, material, composed of the four elements, and feeding on solid food.

Poṭṭhapāda sees this body as the self, "me." The Buddha responds:

But with such a gross self, Poṭṭhapāda, perception would be one thing, and the self another. You can see it in this way. Given such a gross self, certain perceptions would arise in a person, and others pass away. In this way you can see that perception must be one thing, the self another.

In other words, if Poṭṭhapāda is the gross self, the body, then how does he account for perceptions, which come and go? How can the two be identical?

Poṭṭhapāda seems to concede the truth of this, for he now comes up with another idea. He postulates a mind-made self. Here, too, we can identify with him. People often claim to have accepted the fact: "I am not the body." It is a risky statement, however. A deeper insight would be: "The body is not mine." If we say, "I am not the body," it still implies ownership, and who is that owner? It is, of course, "me." "I" own the body, "I" try to keep it healthy and happy, bring it pleasant sense-contacts. It is mine in the same way as a house, a car, or a refrigerator is mine. I certainly do not think I am the refrigerator. This is Poṭṭhapādaʼs position when he now says:

> Lord, I postulate a mind-made self complete with all its parts, not defective in any sense organ.

He has in no way given up the idea of ownership. All he has done is to substitute the mind for the body. "I am the mind" rather than "I am the body." The Buddha replies as he did before:

> But with such a mind-made self, perception would be one thing, and the self another…. Given such a mind-made self, certain perceptions would arise in a person, and others pass away. In this way you can see that perception must be one thing, the self another.

Forced to see the truth of this, Poṭṭhapāda thinks up yet another possibility, "Lord, I assume a formless self, made up of perception." In fact, he is being quite clever. If the self is neither the body, nor the mind, then perhaps it has no materiality whatsoever; perhaps it is formless. "Formless" is a word used in connection with the higher jhānas, which the Buddha has already explained. Here again he tells Poṭṭhapāda that perception would be one thing, the self another. Even given such a formless self, certain perceptions would arise in a person and others pass away. He is trying to get Poṭṭhapāda to see that logically a perception cannot be the same as a self, formless or not, for perceptions arise, and then they cease. Poṭṭhapāda now asks him:

> But Lord, is it possible for me to know whether perception is a personʼs self, or whether perception is one thing, and self another?

He is growing a little frustrated. The Buddha says:

> Poṭṭhapāda, it is difficult for one of different views, a different faith, under different influences, with different pursuits

and a different training to know whether these are two different things or not.

In other words, he says you are not my student. You have learned from other teachers, have a different belief system, have come under different influences, and so it would be very hard for you to realize this truth.

It is much the same for us today. If we are influenced by a belief in the soul, or the afterlife, or happiness after death, or a particular way of practice, it is indeed difficult for us to understand; we are, so to say, on a different track. Of course we can change our minds; we do so constantly, but we need to see the necessity for that change. In order to truly hear what the Buddha teaches, we need to become so aware of our own dukkha—this is always the first step—that we finally recognize that nothing we have previously tried has been successful in eradicating dukkha. Then, perhaps, we may be ready for a profound change and be influenced in a different way. Later, Poṭṭhapāda himself became a student of the Buddha. At this stage, however, he is still full of all kinds of ideas and theories, which he has come across through various teachers, or from the *Ṛg Veda*, ancient Brahmanic teachings, often committed to memory by spiritual aspirants, with which he was undoubtedly familiar. The Buddha is gently pointing out that, because of Poṭṭhapāda's previous conditioning, it is impossible for him to present the answers to these questions in a way that Poṭṭhapāda can accept. As a result, Poṭṭhapāda now abandons this line of questioning, and this part of their conversation comes to a close. As we shall see in the next chapter, he will begin again, asking totally different questions, but for the moment he is silenced. It is obvious that he is quite unable to get to the absolute truth about the self.

In the last chapter various selves were mentioned, all of which have been postulated at one time or another, culminating in the "unity-self." Poṭṭhapāda has come up with three: body, mind, and formless. He does not yet see that all these statements are just ideas. We are in exactly the same position. We have our own ideas, and we believe them with great vehemence because they are "mine." But are there really solid grounds for them? Just because "I" have an idea about something or someone, does that make it true? On an absolute level, of course, it does not; for on that level all is flux and movement. But even on a relative level, there is no guarantee that this is so. We should always question our ideas and try to see where they come from. If they are negative, we should question them even more. We need to recognize their source, which is always within ourselves. Any idea we have is just a projection. Even the idea of self is a projection, one that we would like to be true because it provides a foundation for our greed and hate. If, however, we have come to realize that these two do not bring us much joy, we may perhaps be able to go a step further than Potṭhapāda. We may be able to see more clearly and wonder how we could ever have imagined there could actually be "somebody" within all that flux of arising and ceasing. Who could possibly be sitting inside, pulling the strings, like a puppet master in a puppet theater, making lifeless dolls dance and hop around? Do we really think we are that somebody? It seems that we do, and we should examine this idea over and over again.

Like Potṭhapāda, we too have encountered different influences. We have been influenced by what others think and by everything we have ever experienced and believed we understood. But the Buddha offers us a training, and within that training we may catch a glimpse of freedom. No longer having a "self" is the only worthwhile freedom because it liberates us from greed and hate. The Buddha's genius lies in the fact that he was capable of explaining to others what he himself had experienced.

# 9

# Disenchantment, Dispassion, and the Four Noble Truths

Poṭṭhapāda now embarks on quite another line of questioning. He is very much like us, is he not? If we cannot grasp the answer to one thing, we drop the whole subject and come up with another.

> Well, Lord, if this question of self and perceptions is difficult for one like me, tell me: Is the world eternal? Is only this true and the opposite false?

The Buddha replies:

> Poṭṭhapāda, I have not declared that the world is eternal, and that the opposite view is false.

The following dialogue ensued:

> "Well, Lord, is the world not eternal?"
> "I have not declared that the world is not eternal."
> "Well, Lord, is the world infinite...not infinite?"
> "I have not declared that the world is not infinite, and that the opposite view is false."

This four-pointed method of questioning, which can seem so cumbersome to us now, is typical of the way debates were conducted in India in Poṭṭhapāda's day: "Is it so? Is it not so? Is it both so and not so? Is it neither so, nor not so?" Using this method, Poṭṭhapāda brings up ten points, which became known as the Undeclared (or Indeterminate) Points. They are the ten points that the Buddha did not declare, questions he was not prepared to answer. Scholars believe that this questionnaire was traditionally put to ascetics, wanderers, and spiritual leaders in order to discover what views they held. The dialogue between Poṭṭhapāda and the Buddha continues:

> "Well, Lord, is the soul the same as the body? ... is the soul one thing and the body another?"
> "I have not declared that the soul is one thing and the body another."
> "Well, Lord, does the Tathāgata exist after death? Is only this true and all else false?"
> "I have not declared that the Tathāgata exists after death."
> "Well, Lord, does the Tathāgata not exist after death? ... both exist and not exist after death? ... neither exist nor not exist after death?"
> "I have not declared that the Tathāgata neither exists nor does not exist after death, and that all else is false."

Poṭṭhapāda finally asks him:

> But, Lord, why has the Lord not declared these things?

The Buddha's answer is highly meaningful:

> Poṭṭhapāda, that is not conducive to the purpose, not conducive to Dhamma, not the way to embark on the holy life; it does not lead to disenchantment, to dispassion, to cessation, to calm, to higher knowledge, to enlightenment, to Nibbāna. That is why I have not declared it.

He refuses to talk of things that are not relevant to the spiritual path, which cannot help us in dealing with our dukkha.

What possible difference can it make to Poṭṭhapāda if the world is or is not eternal? How can it affect his happiness to know whether the soul is the same as the body? What does it matter whether the Buddha exists after death or not? None of this will get Poṭṭhapāda out of his dukkha, and so the Buddha simply declines to discuss any such questions with him.

This sequence occurs elsewhere in the suttas also, for others posed similar questions. Vacchagotta, a wanderer of a different faith, was one. He came to the Buddha and asked him whether the *Tathāgata* (an epitaph the Buddha used for himself) existed after death or not? Did he neither exist nor not exist? Did he both exist and not exist? The Buddha said he declared none of this. Then how, Vacchagotta asked, can I possibly understand this? The Buddha's answer was to tell Vacchagotta to go and collect some firewood, and make a fire. He then asked him to throw more and more sticks on it, which Vacchagotta did. The Buddha asked him how the fire was going and was told it was burning very well. Now, the Buddha said, stop throwing sticks on it. After a little while, he again asked Vacchagotta how the fire was behaving? It's going out was the answer. After another look: It's gone out completely. You see, the Buddha told him, that is exactly what happens to the Tathāgata. Where did the fire go? Did it go forward or backward, sideways, to the right, to the left? No, said Vacchagotta. It just went out. Well, the Buddha persisted, did it go up or did it go down? No, Vacchagotta replied, it simply went out because there was no more fuel. That is right, said the Buddha, and the Tathāgata too just goes out, for there is no more fuel for his passions.

The same question is still being asked today, though not in those words, of course. Within certain traditions, in countries where Buddhism has taken root, there are all kinds of ideas about what happened to the Buddha after death. But he himself said quite clearly that if the fire of the passions is no longer fueled, then mind and body have nothing to feed on and just go out. We really do not need to debate that point, either with others or in our own minds.

The Buddha, as he told Poṭṭhapāda, did not answer questions about things that were "not conducive to the purpose...not conducive to Dhamma." There is a nice story in another sutta, that illustrates this. A man is hit in the chest by an arrow and collapses. Gravely wounded, he is on the brink of death, so a doctor is summoned to remove the arrowhead. But the man will not let him do this. First, he wants to know from what kind of wood the arrow shaft is made; then he wants to find out what sort of poison had been put on its tip; and what kind of feathers were attached to its end; were they goose feathers or hawk feathers? He wants to know what the arrowhead was made of, and who shot the arrow at him, and from what distance, and why? Naturally, by the time he finds all that out, he dies. The story represents our tendency to ask questions about all sorts of unimportant details instead of practicing those things that will lead us out of dukkha. In the story, the arrow is dukkha, the Buddha is the doctor, and the cure is the Dhamma. The man refused to receive the Dhamma unless he was given all kinds of extraneous and useless information first.

The Buddha is saying the same thing to Poṭṭhapāda. None of the questions you are asking have any bearing on what should actually be done. But Poṭṭhapāda is not ready to "do" anything. He is plainly fascinated by the Buddha, for otherwise he would not be detaining him so long with all these questions, but he is still only involved on an intellectual level. The Buddha, however, must have felt that here was somebody capable of learning; this is fortunate for us, for otherwise, without Poṭṭhapāda's questions, we would not have the Buddha's lengthy explanations.

Answering these questions, the Buddha says, does not lead to disenchantment, to dispassion, to cessation, to calm, to higher knowledge, to enlightenment, nor to Nibbāna. Disenchantment is an important step on the way to enlightenment, part of the sequence known as "transcendental dependent arising," which starts with the acknowledgment of our own suffering, which causes confidence in the teaching and joy that we are able to practice. Then comes *sammā samādhi* (right concentration), meditation itself. This brings us the "knowledge and vision of things as they really are," in other words, the insight that everything is impermanent, unsatisfactory, and without substance. This then leads to disenchantment with the world, and it is this disenchantment, which is the necessary first step for leading us out of dukkha. Until then, we are only familiarizing ourselves with the practice. We cannot give ourselves to it wholeheartedly while we still look to the world for our fulfillment, while we still believe that finding the right person, job, place to live, or whatever it may be, is the answer to our woes. Until we get to the point of disenchantment, we will practice halfheartedly, at best, which will, of course, bring halfhearted results. What else could it do?

Naturally we have to live in this world. We have bodies, and in order to stay alive, they need oxygen, sunshine, rain, food, and many other things. But inner fulfillment is never dependent on anything exterior. We cannot pipe it in from the outside, for there is no pipeline. Fulfillment can only come to us from within.

It may take us quite a while to understand this truth. Some people arrive at it very quickly, others take longer, and there are those who never see it at all. It depends to a great extent on our *karmic* resultants, and on our opportunities, which are, of course, themselves karmic resultants.

Disenchantment does not mean that we dislike the world, or the people in it, or nature around us, or the myriad things we use and live with. Disenchantment is not disgust, though sometimes it is wrongly translated as such. Disgust has a negative connotation, and as soon as we have negativity within, our practice is already marred. We are not disgusted with the world; we simply no longer attach such great importance to all the things we can do with our bodies, or relate to with our minds. We stop looking to the world for absolute fulfillment. This does not usually happen until we have already looked there repeatedly. It is rare therefore to arrive at disenchantment while we are very young, though it can of course happen. Most of us, however, have to experience what the world has to offer and be disappointed by it many times before we even start to look for a different path to happiness.

Having come to meditation, however, does not necessarily mean that we have also experienced disenchantment. Many of us take up meditation because we want to add something pleasurable to our lives. The Buddha said that this was better than not practicing at all. He was happy for each person who came to him and asked questions. Here we can observe him giving very direct and succinct answers to Poṭṭhapāda; don't think about all these external things, think about how to arrive at disenchantment. If we start to meditate just because we want to experience something more refined in our lives, that too will eventually work for us if we remain steadfast in our meditation and persevere with it. If, through the jhānas, we can see that there is a totally different level of consciousness available, even to ordinary people such as ourselves, we may finally understand that the world offers us only fool's gold. It glitters, but it has no value. It does indeed shine most temptingly. Beautiful women, handsome men, fine weather, delicious food; the music sounds wonderful, the books are fascinating—but all is dependent on our sense-contacts. It is all out there, exterior to us, and cannot touch our deepest being. In Pali, it is known as *māra*, temptation.

We are constantly tempted by the world, not only because it looks so inviting, but because everybody else seems to think that is where happiness lies. Some appear to be doing very well, to have all they want, and we wonder: "Why do they seem so pleased with their lives, when I am not? Maybe I should do what they are doing," and we try it out. If we keep trying things out in this way for too long, we will miss the opportunity offered us in this lifetime to follow an inner path. To arrive at disenchantment requires quite a lengthy amount of practice, and that is still only the very first step of the in-depth realization of the Dhamma.

After disenchantment comes dispassion, which is the springboard for the experience of Nibbāna. At this stage, our disenchantment has grown so strong that, when greed or hate arise, we are able to drop them immediately, but they have not disappeared. Greed and hate are only lost completely at the last stage before enlightenment, and even then they hover in the background in a subtle way, though they no longer disturb us. Only the arahant, the Enlightened One, is entirely safe from them. With dispassion, however, we no longer want to grasp and cling, or reject and resist. The underlying tendency is still there, but we are able to let it go because we have seen the truth that lies in disenchantment. Unless we do so, we will not be able to continue on our spiritual journey.

Disenchantment and dispassion are vital steps on this path. It is worth repeating here that they cannot happen until we have recognized our own dukkha. If we simply want to add a little meditation to our lives, we can never come anywhere near either of them. Recognizing dukkha does not mean we have to experience some great tragedy. Dukkha is the constant feeling of restlessness, anxiety, and disquiet, not being quite at ease. When we recognize dukkha, confidence in the teaching arises. This means we are then willing to commit ourselves, not to a blind belief in the Buddha's words, but to finding out whether what he said is true on all its levels. With that commitment comes the joy of being able to do something that goes far beyond our worldly endeavors, and it is that joy that makes it possible to meditate. Then, as we have seen, in this cause-and-effect sequence of "transcendental dependent arising," the next steps are the meditative absorptions, followed by "knowledge and vision of things as they really are," which is the understood experience of impermanence, unsatisfactoriness, and corelessness.

To experience something does not mean that we necessarily understand it. In daily life, we can get by with a minimum of understanding in just the same way as we can skim through a newspaper even if our vocabulary is limited. Our everyday life does not demand any profound insights from us; it is enough if we handle things with a certain amount of efficiency. Whereas, if we wish to follow the Buddha's teaching, we must go much deeper; become aware of each present moment and its significance, and truly understand what we experience.

As we do this, we begin to see impermanence as a way of life; we are that impermanence. This goes far beyond a simple acceptance of the fact that everything is impermanent, or that our breath is impermanent. We recognize it as a truth about ourselves at the deepest level of our being.

In just the same way, we recognize the truth of dukkha, as we experience, over and over again, the underlying disquiet in our minds and hearts. We become aware of how much time we spend trying to find external causes, putting the blame on somebody else. It has to be somebody else's fault. We completely forget, at these moments, that the other person has the same disquiet, in exactly the same way as we have it. Instead, all we see is that we are not peaceful and then produce a list of possible reasons for that. None of this goes to the depth of our being, but stays on the surface, just touching the rim of our experience.

It is of great importance to become aware of impermanence and dukkha, not just in ourselves, but wherever we look. Every tree, every bush, every leaf, every blade of grass speaks loudly of impermanence. Each single day is totally imbued with it. Perhaps we own one of those digital clocks, which blink off and on each second. Nothing could reveal impermanence more plainly. Yet somehow we always have the idea that, although the clock is moving, we are standing still. How could that possibly be? We are exactly the same as the clock, we are going with it.

Dispassion makes a great impact on the way we lead our lives. But it can only come about as a result of our previous practice, all is cause and effect. Sometimes, because we have been able to let go of a particular desire, we believe that we have already reached a state of dispassion. Then we are surprised when the next desire arises. Of course it is commendable, indeed important, to let go of a desire, but that is not to be rid of passion. We are still involved with desire, still having to practice. In the story about Vacchagotta the fire only goes out when there is no more fuel at all. Some people may say, but I like my passions. I want to keep them. If we feel that way, then we will simply have to wait until a change takes place in us; it may be in this life, the next life, a hundred lives from now, who knows? It could even be tomorrow. We change our mind when we approach things differently. The better the meditation works, the clearer the mind can see the reality in which we live. Most people live in a reality they have invented. They imagine it to be as they would like it to be. Then they wonder why they are not happy, which is simply because imagination and reality do not coincide. Our inner being cannot be arranged to suit our desires, we cannot buy our own reality. If we could, every rich person would be completely content, which has never yet happened. Some of them, indeed, are so desperately miserable that they commit suicide. We probably know all this, at some level of our being. But do we act on it? What we know and what we do are often miles apart. This is an important aspect of the spiritual life. If we truly know something, we must act upon it. Otherwise it leads us nowhere. Knowledge alone cannot bring about change.

Dispassion, as the Buddha says in this sutta, leads to "cessation, calm, and higher knowledge." As long as the mind has hate and greed, it cannot go beyond itself. It is caught in its own whirlpool of reactions. We can often actually feel this when our thoughts turn around in an endless circle, over and over again. We are just like Poṭṭhapāda, with his flurry of ideas and opinions. As long as we still harbor hate and greed and allow them to come to the fore in our meditation, we can never be calm or experience the higher states of consciousness. The mind is then still too connected to the world. In meditation, it is a question of calming the mind, so that it is able to see the world as simply a necessary foundation for the body, not as something that does or does not bring us happiness, and certainly not as something that needs our attention at that time. Of course, when we are confronted by people or situations, we must concern ourselves with the world, but for the period of meditation we need to step out of the eddies stirred up in us by greed and hate. Only then will we reach the higher jhānas and the higher knowledge, or *abhiññā*, which means the loss of our hindrances and underlying tendencies. By the time we come to this point on our spiritual journey, these will have dissolved to such an extent that they are no longer an obstruction to us.

The Buddha had four ways of answering questions: with a simple yes or no; with a lengthy explanation, as in this sutta; with a counterquestion, which also occurs here, as we shall see; and lastly with silence. Rather than remaining silent, he has told Poṭṭhapāda why he is not prepared to answer all his questions. It would not be conducive to the purpose, and that, he says, is why I have not declared it. At this, Poṭṭhapāda comes up with another question. After all, the Buddha is the teacher, and so quite rightly, he asks him:

But, Lord, what has the Lord declared?

The Buddha answers:

Poṭṭhapāda, I have declared: "This is suffering, this is the origin of suffering, this is the cessation of suffering, and this is the path leading to the cessation of suffering."

These are the Four Noble Truths, the essence of the Buddha's teaching. Poṭṭhapāda had gone off on too many tangents, pursuing ideas that are not helpful, so the Buddha is leading him back to these basic truths. They are the Buddha's enlightenment statement. He had sat for a week in the meditative absorptions, under the famous Bodhi Tree in what is today Bodhgaya. When he came out of meditation, he formulated these Noble Truths and realized that they were the answer to humankind's dilemma. After his enlightenment, he explained them in his very first discourse, the *Dhammacakka-pavattana Sutta* (*Dhammacakka* is "the wheel of the Dhamma" and *pavattana* is "turning"), to five friends with whom he had previously studied under two meditation teachers. On hearing this exposition, one of the five immediately became enlightened. Later, the others followed suit. They became the first Buddhist monks, disciples, and followers of the Buddha.

The path leading to the cessation of suffering is the Noble Eightfold Path, which is divided into three parts: *sīla, samādhi,* and *paññā* (morality, concentration, and wisdom), all of which are addressed in this discourse. Poṭṭhapāda has heard about the necessity to live a moral life; he has heard about the jhānas, or concentration; and wisdom was touched on when he raised questions about the existence or nonexistence of a "self." In fact, Poṭṭhapāda is still of the opinion that there is a self and will bring the matter up again later. He does not change his mind until the very end of the discourse, when he becomes a disciple of the Buddha. The teaching of the Buddha always contains all three parts; if not, it is incomplete. Indeed, any spiritual teaching that is worth following has to embrace morality, concentration, and wisdom. Instead of concentration—the usual translation for samādhi—we could call it tranquility, serenity, or calm. A calm mind can gain wisdom.

Poṭṭhapāda still has a question:

> But, Lord, why has the Lord declared this?

Very patiently, the Buddha repeats what he said before:

> Because, Poṭṭhapāda, this is conducive to the purpose, conducive to Dhamma, the way to embark on the holy life; it leads to disenchantment, to dispassion, to cessation, to calm, to higher knowledge, to enlightenment, to Nibbana. That is why I have declared it.

At that, Poṭṭhapāda seems to finally understand, for he says:

> So it is, Lord, so it is, Well-Farer. And now is the time for the Blessed Lord to do as he sees fit.

Then the Lord rose from his seat and went away.

The message that Poṭṭhapāda was left with is as relevant today as it was then, namely, it is only useful to enquire into matters that are conducive to our spiritual development. Among the Brahmins, the priests, and spiritual teachers in India at that time, as they still are today, long discussions are often recorded; discourses about whether the world is eternal or not, whether it is finite or not, whether the soul is or is not identical with the body. Yet if we reflect on this, we will see that none of this could be of any help to us in our practice. On the contrary, it would merely create more discursive thinking. It certainly could not lead to concentration.

The most useful enquiry we can make is to look into the Four Noble

Truths and to experience them within ourselves. The first two, that there is suffering and that its origin lies in craving, or attachment and aversion, can be experienced at almost any moment of any day. If we are able to realize these truths, we may then be able to take the third, the cessation of suffering, on trust for the time being. The fourth truth, the pathway out of suffering, which is the Eightfold Path, eventually leads to that freedom. It is of great importance to enquire into these truths until we really understand them. "Do I experience dukkha? If so, am I blaming an outside source? Do I still believe that something or someone is causing my suffering? Or am I completely convinced, from my own experience, that I myself cause it?" If we are not quite certain of this, we must keep asking ourselves the same question. "Who is causing my dukkha?" Of course we can intellectualize it: "Nobody is interested in causing me dukkha, no one cares enough to do so," or any other rationalization we care to make; but that is of little help. We have to recognize this truth within ourselves and react accordingly. Once we do so and are able to drop whatever our desire may be at that time, we will see that dukkha instantly vanishes too.

Our desire may be quite a worthy one. Perhaps we want to have a good meditation. But as long as we are thinking like that, can we meditate? Of course not. Nothing happens at all. If there is an "I want," there will be dukkha. Suppose we drop the wanting, let it go? Suppose we sit down, cross our legs, and are simply there, in the present moment, with no wants? We will discover how well that works. Anyone can experience this. Even if our minds are still a whirlpool, we can all let the craving go for just a few seconds and become aware of the great relief that brings. It is a moment of truth. We lose a burden, as if we had been carrying a heavy rucksack and are at last able to put it down. Of course the untrained mind picks it up again almost immediately, but we can drop it over and over again. As we do so, we will not only become quite efficient at letting go of our craving, but we will see the results: expansiveness, openness, ease, lightness, meditation.

The more wholeheartedly we can give ourselves to the meditation, desiring nothing from it, the better. We would be wise, too, to clear our minds of those speculative, purely intellectual lines of enquiry that the Buddha said were not helpful, and of which Poṭṭhapāda is so fond. Poṭṭhapāda's questions are of value in order to show us what is useful for spiritual development and what is not.

## 10

# The Cessation of Craving:
# What is Conducive to Nibbāna

In the last chapter Poṭṭhapāda ended his conversation with the Buddha with the words, "So it is, Lord." But no sooner had the Buddha left the debating-hall than Poṭṭhapāda's fellow-wanderers turned on him:

> Then the wanderers, as soon as the Lord had left, reproached, sneered and jeered at Poṭṭhapāda from all sides, saying: "Whatever the ascetic Gotama says, Poṭṭhapāda agrees with him: 'So it is, Lord, so it is, Well-Farer.' We don't understand a word of the ascetic Gotama's whole discourse: 'Is the world eternal or not? Is it finite or infinite? Is the soul the same as the body or different? Does the Tathāgata exist after death or not, or both, or neither?'"

Poṭṭhapāda answers:

> I don't understand either about whether the world is eternal or not...or whether the Tathāgata exists after death or not, or both, or neither. But the ascetic Gotama teaches a true and real way of practice which is consonant with Dhamma and grounded in Dhamma.

It is interesting that they refer to him as "the ascetic Gotama" rather than "the Buddha," the name by which, at that time, he had long been known. They seem to imply he was simply one of them, an ascetic or wanderer. Also, Poṭṭhapāda uses the word Dhamma, by which we usually mean the teaching of the Buddha. But Poṭṭhapāda is not yet a disciple of the Buddha, and this is the first time he has heard the teaching. The word was already in use, and for him and others like him, it denoted something grounded in absolute truth, in the laws of nature. He goes on:

And why should not a man like me express approval of such a true and real practice, so well taught by the ascetic Gotama?

Although not a follower of the Buddha, he has seen that the teaching is of value, and approves of it.

The sutta continues:

> Two or three days later, Citta, the son of the elephant-trainer, went with Poṭṭhapāda to see the Lord. Citta prostrated himself before the Lord and sat down to one side.

So we can assume that Citta had already heard the teaching and was a devotee. Poṭṭhapāda, on the other hand, only exchanged courtesies with the Lord, before sitting down and telling him what had happened, how the other wanderers had mocked him. The Buddha says:

> Poṭṭhapāda, all those wanderers are blind and sightless, you alone among them are sighted.

He often used such images, and once said there are few people "with little dust in their eyes," by which he meant those who could actually understand what he was saying to them. Indeed, after his enlightenment, as he sat under the Bodhi Tree enjoying the bliss of Nibbāna, he decided he would not teach. He felt people would not understand his doctrine because it was so different from anything they might have heard previously and from what they related to in their own lives. The story goes that the highest Brahmā, the foremost of the gods, came to him and begged him to teach for the benefit of gods and men. Then the Buddha saw, perhaps as an inner vision, that there were those who had "little dust in their eyes," and decided that, for their sake, he would become a teacher. Now he continues:

> Some things I have taught and pointed out, Poṭṭhapāda, as being certain, others as being uncertain. Which are the things I have pointed out as uncertain?

The Buddha repeats the list: whether the world is eternal or not, whether it is infinite or not, whether the soul is the same as the body or not, and whether the Tathāgata exists after death or not, or both exists and not exists, or neither exists nor not exists.

> Why? Because they are not...conducive to Nibbāna. That is why I have declared them as uncertain.

Once again, he is making it clear that he only teaches that which leads to final liberation. No matter where we look in his teaching, it goes in one direction only. That was not always understood in his time and certainly not taught by many teachers.

It is the same today. Our journey leads us step by step to one goal, Nibbāna. It does not lead to annihilation. There is nothing of that in Nibbāna; there is only clarity, complete and utter knowing, the end of all illusion. This knowing, however, is not omniscience. The Buddha once said he could not know everything simultaneously; but where he put his mind, that he knew. To reach Nibbāna is not to have acquired some kind of omnipotence, with which to make a great impression on the world. Rather, it is the end of delusion, and the end of dukkha.

> But what things have I pointed out as certain? "This is suffering, this is the origin of suffering, this is the cessation of suffering, this is the path leading to the cessation of suffering." Why? Because they are conducive to the purpose, conducive to Dhamma, the way to embark on the holy life; they lead to disenchantment, to dispassion, to cessation, to calm, to higher knowledge, to enlightenment, to Nibbana. That is why I have declared them as certain.

He is bringing Poṭṭhapāda back to the Four Noble Truths, enumerating the steps that are needed for insight, each one leading to the next, until one can finally let go of all illusion.

We have already looked at disenchantment and dispassion. Next comes cessation, a word that has several different connotations. It can mean cessation of perception and feeling, which occurs in the ninth jhāna.

In the context of Nibbāna, it can also mean the cessation of all suffering, all illusion. As the Buddha uses it here, it refers to the three cravings that, as a result of dispassion, cease to arise. They are the desire for sensual gratification, the craving for existence, and the craving for nonexistence. These three are the underlying causes for our being here, for the human condition. We are often tempted to blame our parents for the way we behave and for their effect on us. Parents are not usually enlightened beings and may well do unwise things. But it is our own craving that brought us here, into our particular family, and this craving is something we need to investigate.

Desire for sensual gratification has been mentioned at some length, and if we have looked into ourselves, we will already have seen the truth of it. But the craving for existence goes even deeper. It is the strongest desire we have, the one that constantly pushes us around. In our daily lives we are probably quite unaware of it. People often keep themselves busy simply to avoid seeing the unsatisfactoriness of the human condition. This is a common way of dealing with dukkha. But if we really look at the craving for existence, really get a feeling for what that means, then we will know what the Buddha taught, because that craving creates continuous dukkha.

It makes us grasp for things to fill the mind, that is why we think. It makes us move, to get away from whatever it is we do not like. Reflect for a moment on how our beds usually look in the morning: disordered, rumpled, bedding all over the place. The mind still experiences dukkha, even in sleep, so we move about. When we wake, what is our first thought? Are we thinking: "Isn't it marvelous to be alive!"? How rare such a person is. For most of us, it is more likely to be: "Here we go again," or words to that effect. How many of us are aware of the way we actually come out of sleep? How consciousness arises, how it instantly wants to be filled with happenings, which we then create? Otherwise it would be too boring, we say, and we look around for things to do. But all this activity is nothing more than a means of supporting the illusion that there is an "I," who is busy and therefore really important. It feeds our craving to be. Everything we do, in fact, is directed toward that end. If we were to examine ourselves closely, we would soon see how true this is. Even our best, most well-intentioned actions are still a support system for our craving for existence.

It is helpful to examine one whole day in all detail. It could be today, though that can sometimes be difficult, because we are too close to it. We might take the previous day and try to remember how we spent each moment. "What was I doing? How did I occupy my mind? How did I keep that illusion of self going? Can I recognize, in that constant movement, the craving for existence?" The movement is not only physical, but mental as well. Our minds latch on to this and that; we think of what we could do in the future, what we have done in the past. It is only when we are thinking that we know we are existing. All this mental activity serves one purpose—to support the craving to be. In meditation, through using a meditation subject such as the breath, we learn to let go of discursive thinking. If we can let go of it then, we can do so in daily life as well. As we do so, calm and tranquility arise.

The craving for nonexistence is just the other side of the same coin. It is rooted in the same delusion, namely that there is a "me." In this case the "me" does not want to be here. Everything seems terrible, and "I" want to get out of it. This is the "longing-not-to-be," and it is just as much of an obstacle to the experience of Nibbāna as is the craving to be. If we have understood dukkha and are now willing to investigate the craving for existence, we must be careful not to fall into this trap. For if we come to the conclusion that things are unsatisfactory and full of suffering, we may want to escape from all that, which is in itself another form of craving. It is still "I" wanting to "get" something. This can never work. What is needed is just the opposite; to let go of everything that makes up this illusion, which we take for reality. It is the practice of seeing things again and again as they are and not as we believe them to be. As long as we are enmeshed in our beliefs and preconceptions, we can make no progress. It is like the wanderers who reproached Poṭṭhapāda and made fun of him. They do not want to hear anything new. Poṭṭhapāda does, but so far he has not quite caught on to what he should be doing.

It is important to investigate the three cravings and their possible cessation; to contemplate them deeply. This can be done at any time during a formal meditation period, or just sitting on a tree stump, or even as we walk.

The next step mentioned by the Buddha is calm. We can learn to drop the restless thinking, which prevents us from experiencing calm and tranquillity. Often, during the day, we think, even when there is really nothing that needs pondering. We simply bring up a thought because we need something to occupy our mind. If we can catch ourselves doing that, which is not so difficult, we can practice letting the thought go, and thereby experience a state of bare awareness, where there is only pure, translucent mind. We can just be. At such moments there is inner peace, which is also conducive to restoring energy. Thinking is hard and tiring work. We may have a job that makes no greater physical demands than pressing a few buttons or pushing a pen around, but at the end of the day we are worn out because we had to think, assess, and react without pause. But none of us have to think when it is not necessary to do so.

We will not find this easy to achieve. The calm state of bare awareness only comes about as a result of the cessation of craving for existence. But before the craving can cease, we have to realize its implications. We have to recognize its constant manifestation and how unsatisfactory it is, how restless and agitated it makes us, even though we may not outwardly appear so. There is a continuous feeling of inner unrest, which we often try to rationalize and pin on some outer cause. But there is only one cause and that is the craving for existence.

When we see that for ourselves, it is another "Ah ha!" experience. The calm mind, which has been meditating well, can observe this more easily, for it can remain objective. Subjectively, we say, "This is me, and I've so much to do. It takes up too much time, but if I don't do it, nobody else will" or similar thoughts. Objectively, though, it is possible simply to see a person acting and performing, following an inner drive. All of it is the craving for existence, no matter where that drive leads us. The difficulty lies in exactly that paradox. We need the drive in order to do the practice, to investigate, contemplate, and understand the Buddha's teaching. But we have to let go of it in order to attain Nibbāna. There has to be a switch. It is as if we moved from one set of rails to another. But we can only do this when we have investigated ourselves so deeply that we know every facet of what is going on within us. Not that there is anything to be disliked, blamed, or resented. There is nothing we should feel guilty about. Everything within us is part of human nature, which we can transcend, but first we have to be aware of the underlying causes. Contemplating our basic craving for existence is extremely interesting. It is quite difficult to do, but then things that are easy do not usually produce important results.

After cessation and calm, the Buddha mentions the next step, which is higher knowledge. Again, this can have different connotations, but the most important one is that the person who has been practicing knows that the hindrances, together with their underlying tendencies, have now been abandoned. This cannot happen until the craving for existence has also been abandoned. The hindrances are part and parcel of our human make-up. As we practice the path of purification, we can chip away at them and lessen their power over us. For this, our support systems are concentration in meditation, mindfulness, and substituting the unwholesome with the wholesome. But we cannot lose them entirely that way. Greed and hate will still be there. Only at the last stage on the spiritual path will we finally be capable of letting them go entirely. Subsequent to higher knowledge comes enlightenment, Nibbāna, the very last step on the journey. The Buddha uses both words here, but they are identical in meaning, and this was probably simply a turn of phrase.

The path to enlightenment through meditation and purification clarifies the mind to such an extent that it is able to investigate the deepest underlying foundation of our being. This foundation is revealed as nothing other than the craving for existence. It is the linchpin that makes us do the most foolish, dramatic, and terrible things, but it is also what makes us do just those ordinary things we always do, in our everyday life, from morning to night.

The Buddha has now twice repeated his teaching to Poṭṭhapāda, telling him of the pathway of insight leading to Nibbāna and the Four Noble Truths. But he knows very well that Poṭṭhapāda has still not really grasped it, so he now puts it in rather different terms:

Poṭṭhapāda, there are some ascetics and Brahmins who declare and believe that after death the self is entirely happy and free from disease.

This is the familiar notion of Paradise, where we play a harp and are blissful forever. It has to be said that this idea is still current in some Buddhist circles; that, for instance, by chanting the name of the next Buddha, we will be reborn in the Pure Land where we will always be happy.

I approached them and asked if this was indeed what they declared and believed, and they replied: "Yes." Then I said:

"Do you, friends, living in the world, know and see it as an entirely happy place?" and they replied: "No." I said: "Have you ever experienced a single night or day, or half a night or day, that was entirely happy?" and they replied: "No."

The Buddha is not only showing Poṭṭhapāda that the Brahmins are declaring unsubstantiated facts, he is also pointing out that anyone who believes we can find happiness in this world is on the wrong track. Obviously, he would like Poṭṭhapāda to investigate this. I would suggest that we also do so. We may reflect on the day just passed or the one we are presently experiencing, just as we did when we contemplated the craving for existence. If we can see how we constantly remove ourselves from one thing because it is not satisfying and go to the next thing, then try to get away from that thing too for the same reason, we will understand the Buddha's question: Have you ever had an entirely happy day or night?

This does not mean we must be unhappy, though of course we may sometimes be that too; but if we examine a perfectly ordinary day, what do we find? It is not totally satisfying, not totally fulfilling. There may be moments of joy, but how long do they last? How often is there an emotion or thought that is not conducive to calm, cessation, or Nibbāna? That is dukkha. It is not dukkha in the obvious sense, the one we can all recognize—the suffering that comes from not getting what we want, or getting what we don't want. It is the dukkha inherent simply in being alive, and we should scrutinize it as closely as we can.

Not that this is intended, in any way, to produce disgust with life. What it results in, if we see it correctly, is an acceptance of life's unsatisfactoriness, and an understanding that the Buddha found the absolute solution. It may also bring a determination to follow in his footsteps and see his truth for ourselves. Becoming aware of that little, niggling discontent that goes on continually in mind and emotions will lessen our dukkha, for we will be able to accept that this is just the way life is. The usual reaction to dukkha is to suffer and lament, but that does not help at all. When we are suffering we cannot see things straight. Therefore, it is very useful to contemplate a whole day, just as it comes, and ask ourselves, what is my mind doing? What does it mean to be alive? The Buddha says that he next asked the Brahmins and ascetics:

Do you know a path or a practice whereby an entirely happy world might be brought about? and they replied: "No."

Today we have countless esoteric magazines and an untold variety of teachings pronouncing theories and ideas about how this might be done, and obviously none of them work. As long as there is craving for existence, there must be dukkha. Specifically, within the craving, lies the fear of annihilation, of nonexistence. Often this manifests as the fear of death. People sometimes say, "Oh, I don't mind dying," because they imagine it is going to be an easy transition. Then they say: "I just don't want to suffer," or "I just don't want my loved ones to die before me." But fear of death is a very real dukkha, hidden in the craving for existence.

The fear of annihilation manifests, too, when we are not valued, accepted, and loved. Some of us will do almost anything in order to be appreciated by others. It makes for a very unsatisfactory life because we become utterly dependent on other people's opinions and emotions, which are never reliable. But because we think we are somebody unique and separate, we need a support system for this person, and when we are unable to find it in ourselves, we try to get it from others. This will always be unsuccessful in the long run, though, of course, we may sometimes receive the love and appreciation we crave. None of us, however, will be given it all the time. Yet the "me," because it is based on an illusion, needs constant support. The bigger the illusion, the more dangerous is the craving. I like to compare it to a very fat person trying to get through a rather small door, bumping into the frame on both sides. In the same way, if we have a great need of ego support, we will feel bruised at the slightest criticism or lack of understanding. The bigger the ego, the more easily it bruises. The smaller the ego, the less difficulties we encounter. When there is none, we cannot be hurt at all. How do we set about reducing the ego? By contemplation, by gaining some insight into the daily, hourly, minute-by-minute manifestation of our craving for existence.

All of us experience a lot of dukkha, although we mostly do not know its underlying cause. Often we see the spiritual path as the way in which to relieve our suffering by doing, saying, or experiencing something that brings happiness. In German we call that: *Friede, Freude, Eierkuchen,* or "peace, joy, and pancakes!" But that is not the Buddha's way. He said the only way to be truly happy is by getting rid of the self-illusion, which means, ultimately, losing the craving for existence.

The Buddha continues:

> I said: "Have you heard the voices of deities who have been reborn in an entirely happy world, saying: 'The attainment of an entirely happy world has been well and rightly gained, and we, gentlemen, have been reborn in such a realm?'" and they replied: "No." What do you think, Poṭṭhapāda? Such being the case, does not the talk of those ascetics and Brahmins turn out to be stupid?

The Buddha had no qualms about saying that a wrong teaching was stupid. He did not believe in supporting any kind of spiritual guidance that did not go to the heart of the matter. This is not the only discourse where he criticizes other teachings, calling them foolish, particularly when they would mislead others.

He now gives a simile:

> It is just as if a man were to say: "I am going to seek out and love the most beautiful girl in the country." They might say to him: "Well as to this most beautiful girl in the country, do you know whether she belongs to the Khattiya, the Brahmin, the merchant or the artisan class?" and he would say: "No." Then they might say: "Well, do you know her name, her clan, whether she is tall or short or of medium height, whether she is dark or light-complexioned or sallow-skinned, or what village or town or city she comes from?" and he would say "No." And they might say: "Well then, you don't know or see the one you seek for and desire?" and he would say: "No." Does not the talk of that man turn out to be stupid?

Poṭṭhapāda replies:

> Certainly, Lord.

It seems he has gained more confidence in the Buddha's teaching, for he now calls him "Lord."

"And so it is with those ascetics and Brahmins who declare and believe that after death the self is entirely happy and free from disease…. Does not their talk turn out to be stupid?"
"Certainly, Lord."

The Buddha wants Poṭṭhapāda to see that these teachers do not have the slightest evidence of anything that might support such a belief. It is just foolish talk, and they are as stupid as the man who decides to find the most beautiful girl in the land, but who has no idea of who she is or where she might be found.

This belief in some sort of eventual eternal happiness is found in most religions: if we lead a reasonably good life, do not commit too many sins, then somehow, in the afterlife, the "self" will be happy forever after. The Buddha never subscribed to this. On the contrary, he said that the only road to happiness was to see the self for what it is: a wrong idea, nothing but a mental formation.

He gives another simile:

It is just as if a man were to build a staircase for a palace at a crossroads. People might say to him: "Well now, this staircase for a palace that you are building—do you know whether the palace will face east, or west, or north or south, or whether it will be high, low or of medium height?" and he would say: "No." And they might say: "Well then, you don't know or see what kind of a palace you are building the staircase for?" and he would say: "No." Don't you think that man's talk would turn out to be stupid?
"Certainly, Lord."

In other words, one would be trying to reach some dream palace of happiness, without the slightest concept of how it might be built, or how to get there. The Buddha talks at some length about all this, because he wants to reintroduce Poṭṭhapāda's own misconceptions and theories of the self, which they had discussed earlier. This time he will introduce the subject a little differently. He is endlessly patient with Poṭṭhapāda, explaining the Dhamma in many ways in the hope that he will finally understand. I think we can identify with Poṭṭhapāda, for it is not easy to grasp that this self that sits here, wanting to be happy, is the very one that constantly gets in the way of that happiness. It obstructs our satisfaction, our fulfillment, at every moment, from morning to night.

If we only look at ourselves subjectively, we see a "me." But once we are able to look objectively, we see that this is nothing but an idea, a mental formation. Not that it is easy to get rid of an ingrained thought pattern, as anyone who meditates knows. But at least we have a handle on it. We begin to see what causes all our ups and downs, our agitation and unrest, why we incessantly desire or reject things. It is the self-illusion, born of the craving for existence. As we come nearer this truth, we see what a genius the Buddha was. In the whole history of humankind, it is the only time that the human condition and the transcending consciousness have been so explicitly outlined.

Many people are devoted to the Buddha, pray to him, but never come to understand his true genius. To have the opportunity of doing so in this lifetime is a karmic resultant of great significance. It is a chance we should seize. To realize the genius of this teaching, which goes to the very foundation of our existence, means we are able to see its truth in ourselves, we "in-see" it. When we can do that, we have understood the Dhamma. This does not mean we have got rid of the "self," but we have apprehended it. Until we know it for what it is, we will never be able to lose it, for in order to let something go, it must first be truly in our grasp.

# 11

# Removing the Illusion of Self

The Buddha now returns to the problem of defining the self, which gave Poṭṭhapāda so much trouble earlier on:

> Poṭṭhapāda, there are three kinds of "acquired self": the gross acquired self, the mind-made acquired self, the formless acquired self.

The word "acquired" can be misunderstood, but the meaning becomes clearer if we think of it as an "assumed" self—the way we assume ourselves to be.

> What is the gross acquired self? It has form, is composed of the four great elements, nourished by material food.

Obviously, that is the body. It is also likened to the realm of sensual desire, the *kāma-loka*. *Kāma* is "desire," and *loka* is "place" or "location." This is the realm we live in, and so desire is constantly with us, part of our makeup, and gives us a great deal of trouble. To transcend it demands hard work and is only possible if we see clearly enough the dukkha it brings us. Eventually we can reach a point where, though we are still in the same location, the same world, we are no longer in the realm of desire.

We, like Poṭṭhapāda, think of this gross acquired self as who we actually are. We have ambivalent feelings about the body; when it is in pain, falls sick, or behaves in ways that are contrary to our wishes, we dislike it very much. When it is in good health, and providing us with many pleasant sense-contacts, we are quite happy to "be" it. We do not really believe we are the body, rather that we own it; yet we have no difficulty in thinking of ourselves as being this particular person, from head to toe. Not seeing the body realistically is one of our major illusions.

The Buddha taught that the body, with its constant demands, can never be totally fulfilling. He said it was the carrier of our senses and necessary to us in the human realm, but we should look on it impersonally, as something we are confronted with, rather than something we own. This idea of ownership is contradicted by everything the body does. No one wants it to fall sick, to hurt, to grow older, and, we must admit, uglier; no one really wants it to die. Yet it does all these things. If we really owned it, why do we have no say in the matter?

The body is made up of the four great elements—earth, fire, water, and air—as is all materiality, and it is kept alive by material food, and that in itself obliges us to deal with a great many demands. If the body were not like this, life would be so much simpler. We would not need toilets, bathtubs, or showers; we would not need a kitchen; we would not have to spend so much of our time and energy buying, growing, or preparing the food our bodies require just to stay alive.

Let us think for a moment of our own homes. What do they contain? Everything is designed for the body. Kitchen, bathroom, bedroom; a living room with comfortable chairs or a couch to sit on. If we live on the upper floors of a building, there is probably an elevator as well, so that the body can be transported without any effort on our part. Wherever we look, we have arranged things for the body's convenience. No wonder we think it is us, or belongs to us.

We demand a great deal of the body, too; it should look just the way we want it to look; not too fat, nor too thin; not too tall, nor too short. It should not have any blemishes, no scratches or wounds, and of course no broken bones. In fact, it should not have anything whatsoever that could possibly bring us the slightest dukkha. But the body refuses to comply, and its presumed owner does not seem to have much control over any of this.

It is well worthwhile taking this question of ownership as a subject of contemplation; perhaps at the end of a meditation period, when our minds are calm and clear. Usually we simply make the assumption: "I am this person." We do not say "I am this body," but think of ourselves as being a particular person, looking a certain way. We need to be more objective and to try to find this assumed owner. We can certainly find the body, all we have to do is look or touch; but who owns it? Perhaps we try to answer by giving the owner a name—it is "me." But what is this "me"? Where is it, how can we find it? When we really go deeply into these questions, we will realize that it is impossible to come up with a logical answer. This, in fact, is what the Buddha will soon explain to Potthapāda, in succinct terms.

It is very hard to convince anyone that the assumption "I am this person" is a fallacy. We look in a mirror and we see "me," and we are really concerned with this "me." We believe our optical illusion, though our optics are extremely limited and only reveal the outer appearance. They can never show us our profound depths. Yet we believe so firmly in the image we see reflected that some of us spend a lot of time on the enhancement of the body. There is total identification. The only way to reveal this fallacy is through calm and insight. The calm mind will, of its nature, gain insight and see things in a different light.

Next, the Buddha describes the second assumed self, which is mind-made:

> What is the mind-made self? It has form, complete with all its parts, not defective in any sense-organ.

This self comes into being when we identify with the observer, with our thoughts, reactions, feelings, sense-contacts. We take the mind to be "me." When we have practiced for some length of time, we often get into difficulties with this idea of an observer, a knower. We should look as deeply as we can, and try to find this one who knows. We will eventually realize that there is no one there. We are simply assuming it, which is why the Buddha calls this an "acquired" self.

This is such a radical teaching that obviously it is not easy to grasp. It runs counter to everything humanity believes in and does. That is why we need to look at the dukkha that arises out of these beliefs. When we see that clearly in ourselves—not in "those poor people out there who don't know what they are doing," but in our own selves—when we actually recognize our own dukkha and its cause, we come nearer to the truth. Everything that we believe in, everything we do, is always geared toward "self" and therefore contains desire, which brings dukkha. When we understand this, we have some inkling of what the Buddha taught.

He himself said it was difficult to take in. We usually look at everything from a standpoint that lies 180 degrees in the opposite direction. Naturally, all our questions then arise out of that opposed viewpoint. That is why, when we hear absolute truths, which is what the Buddha is teaching here, we cannot counter them with questions, which come from the relative level. It is like two separate railway tracks, one of which runs higher up, the other lower down. The two do not meet. For example, people often ask: "If there is no self, and no me, then who is sitting here meditating?" On a relative level, the answer is "me," on an absolute level, it is "nobody."

Of course the Buddha taught on both levels. When he speaks of mindfulness, guarding the sense-doors, clear awareness, morality, he refers to the relative level of a "me" who practices. We must be careful to distinguish between the two levels of the teaching. When he talks about an assumed self, either body or mind, we cannot understand or interpret this with our ordinary, everyday duality outlook. We must either accept what he says and attempt to gain insight through contemplation, or let it go until such time as our practice deepens and our meditation grows strong enough for such an investigation. These are really the only two choices we have. There is a third, which is to disbelieve it. But that is counterproductive and will leave us exactly where we always have been, believing fully and wholeheartedly in "myself."

The latter is a very unsatisfactory standpoint because then we always see "myself" as "here," and the world as "over there." Not only am I an onlooker, an observer, but frequently I am a hostile one too, because the world does not comply with my wishes. Obviously other people have no idea what those wishes might be, and since everyone else is relating in the same ego-based way, we are faced with a universal problem. This creates a duality system, which can be very frightening, for we know ourselves to be mostly powerless. One little person against the whole world; how, we say to ourselves, can we cope with that? When it all gets too much, some of us do indeed stop coping; most of us simply distract ourselves. We keep ourselves busy, so that we have no time to think about it, which is one way of dealing with this threatening outlook. But this does not eliminate decay, disease, and death, nor all our foolish and inappropriate reactions, and it certainly does not eliminate dukkha. That is why the Buddha keeps referring back to the Four Noble Truths. Until we have understood the very first of these—"existence is dukkha"—we have no entry to the path.

Our reactions are almost always dukkha-producing. We react because we believe there is a "me" imprisoned and bounded by our skin, which we want to protect and cherish and often cannot do so. It is this mind-made self that is apparent in all four of the fine-material jhānas, though here the mind-made self is strictly limited to being the observer, and in the fourth, has dwindled to almost nothing.

On the everyday level, this assumed self created by the mind is what all of us experience, in what seems an utterly trustworthy way. Because we all experience it and act on it, over and over, we never really have any doubts about this self, until we come into contact with the inspired depth of the Buddha's teaching. Much of what he has to say here concerns the relative self and learning how to change our negativities into positivities. At this point in the sutta, however, we are confronting the most profound aspect of his teaching.

What is being said here can be found in other religions, but mostly without the explicit guidelines. Mystics through the ages have always known these truths, always tried to express them, usually in terms that conformed to their particular religious faith and may therefore have seemed inaccessible. Also, since the realizations often came to them in a sudden instant of revelation, they found them extremely hard to describe. For these reasons most people have chosen to ignore them, yet they exist in the writings of the Christian mystics of the Middle Ages, the wisdom sayings of Sufi masters, the teachings of Hindu sages, and others. Scholars study such writings, but for the bulk of humanity, the whole subject is meaningless, and they have no interest in it. Instead, they continue to look outside of themselves, rather than inside, in their search for an end to suffering.

Everything we do is an attempt to get out of dukkha. Sometimes that is quite valid, for otherwise our suffering might overwhelm us. But we are not aware that this is our motivation. We have all kinds of ideas and justifications for the things we do: because we have a responsibility; because they need to be done; because they increase our knowledge; because they make others happy. If we were clear on this one point, that we are trying to get out of dukkha, then, even when we do whatever we may have chosen, we would have insight. That is why the Buddha's enlightenment statement is all about dukkha. People often think this to be negative, but he is simply showing us our reality and the way to transcend it.

The Buddha continues:

What is the formless acquired self? It is without form, and made up of perception.

This is the self we deduce from the experience of the higher jhānas, where there is neither physical nor mental form. In the infinities of space and consciousness there is nothing that has any kind of boundary, but there is perception. If that were not so, we would not know we had experienced infinite space and consciousness. We subsequently assume perception to be self.

That is, so to speak, our last resort—perception, awareness, consciousness. If we have renounced the idea of the body as self, or the mind, thoughts, and feelings—even the observer—we are then left with consciousness. "I" am my consciousness. We are still immersed in duality, though this often does not occur to us at the time. There is "my" perception, as opposed to yours. Perhaps "you" can get into the sixth jhāna and have that particular perception, and "I" cannot, so my perception is different from yours. This is again a dualistic viewpoint and can have two possible results, both damaging; either there is a feeling of superiority, "I can do more than you can," or one of inferiority, "I am not as skilled as you are." Both are utterly misplaced.

Consciousness, or perception, simply is. We can use either term, though the word "perception" may be associated in our minds with labeling, as when we practice guarding the sense-doors. What is being addressed here is conscious awareness.

There is a story that illustrates nondualistic perception. A senior monk went for a walk in the forest with some of his juniors. Suddenly a group of bandits leaped out and surrounded them. They told the monks they were going to kidnap one of them so that they could demand a ransom from the monastery for his release. They asked the senior monk to choose which one they should take. He made no answer. They asked him again: "Who shall we take?" But he remained silent. They asked a third time, and there was still no response. At this, they grew angry and said: "Why aren't you answering? What's the matter with you?" He replied, "If I point to one of the junior monks and say you can take him, that would mean I thought him less worthy than the others. If I point to myself, then I am thinking of myself as less worthy. Since there is in fact no distinction between any of us, I cannot point to anyone." This impressed the bandits to such a degree that they left.

As long as we believe in a personal self—an entity, or identity, which is limited, and very dependent on sense-contacts—dukkha will never disappear. This is what the Buddha says now:

> I teach a doctrine for getting rid of the gross acquired self, whereby defiling mental states disappear and states tending to purification grow strong, and one gains and remains in the purity and perfection of wisdom here and now, having realized and attained it by one's own super-knowledge.

He repeats this in exactly the same words for the mind-made, acquired self and the formless acquired self.

To "get rid of" the gross acquired self is often taken to mean annihilation. This is a misunderstanding. In other suttas he says more explicitly, "I teach a doctrine for getting rid of the illusion of the acquired self." It is not that we kill or annihilate something that actually exists; rather, we get rid of a deluded mind-state. Since we are all quite capable of doing that from time to time in daily living, why not get rid of this one?

First, we have to see the necessity for doing so, and that means knowing our own dukkha. Then we have to understand how to go about it. We cannot just say, "All right, I won't any longer believe in a self." It is not possible to lose it in this way. We first have to experience, at least once, what it is like to be without that illusion, and for this to happen, we must be able to meditate.

That is why the Buddha teaches the jhānas, which lead the mind to the point where it can, through concentration and insight into dukkha, actually experience a moment of absolute stillness, a moment when there is no perception, no self-projection. When that moment has occurred, the result is so freeing and liberating, so joyous, filled with such relief, with such a feeling of utter gratitude that we know this to be the truth. But to get there, two things are necessary. Firstly, we have to concentrate. The mind must be one-pointed, not wavering, not wandering off. Secondly, we have to have confidence in our ability to recognize the seed of enlightenment within us. Once we experience full concentration, we will know that this is the most important thing to do in this life and that nothing else can be compared with it.

The Buddha is teaching a doctrine whereby we can get rid of the illusion of self, so that "defiling mental states disappear, and states tending to purification grow strong, and one gains and remains in the purity and perfection of wisdom here and now, having realized and attained it by one's own super-knowledge." Rather than "wisdom," we might use the word "insight," for the two are interchangeable. Or we can say "wisdom-insight." That we come to this wisdom through our own "super-knowledge" is a very important point. Not through rituals, nor through a guru, or a belief system, but strictly through our spiritual growth. The word "super-knowledge" is well-chosen, for it is entirely different from ordinary knowing. It concerns our own experience and being in no doubt whatsoever about its meaning; in other words, the understood experience. The Buddha himself said he was "only the shower of the way." All that any teacher can do is point out the path; it is up to us to walk it.

It is nonetheless true that in the Buddha's lifetime quite a number of people became enlightened after hearing just one of his Dhamma discourses. That was due to the feeling emanating from him. Also, he inspired enormous devotion, which in itself opens the heart. In the East there has always been a much stronger tradition of devotion than in the West, so for us that aspect is perhaps harder. But, though we do not have the advantage of actually hearing the Buddha teach, he has provided so much guidance, in so many discourses, that all we really need to do is follow what he says.

We "realize and attain" this wisdom through our super-knowledge. Realizing means to experience it, and attaining means that we have understood it. Then, the Buddha says, "defiling mental states disappear." Once we have lost the illusion of self, our mental states will no longer revert to negativity. We can check out how rewarding our efforts have been by observing the degree of negativity still present in our own mind-states. This is called "reviewing knowledge."

In the place of defiling mental states, the Buddha says, "states tending to purification grow strong." For it is the illusion of self that gives rise to hate and greed, and once that has disappeared, everything within a person is pure and clear.

The self wants protection, wants opportunities for sensual gratification, and wants to feel safe. Yet we all know there is no safety to be found anywhere in the world. We cannot buy it, though insurance companies grow rich from our efforts to do so. Deep inside, however, we continue to feel just as unsafe as before. Who is it who feels that? The self, of course. Yet, if there is no such self, there is nobody who needs that feeling of safety.

Mind and body just are, and that is all. If we have a great resistance to this doctrine, it simply shows us how strong our attachment to self actually is. What we need then is a little more recognition of our dukkha. As we experience it, the mind will wonder: "Why am I having all this dukkha? It must be the fault of this person or that situation," until finally, one day, we come to the conclusion, "No, it's not. It is actually residing within me."

To follow the Buddha's teaching means to stay with the practice. As we practice, things change, and "states tending to purification grow strong." Purification of mind and heart comes about through "substitution with the opposite," replacing the negative with the positive. Those very unpleasant states of dislike, ill-will, rejection, and resistance, however justified we imagine them to be, create great unhappiness within, and to hold on to them is nothing but foolishness. Once we have learned substitution and can do it well, we will be able to drop whatever is not conducive to happiness.

It is interesting to watch people's faces as we walk along the streets. In any city in the world, it is very difficult to find a happy face. Happiness escapes us because we are in the grip of our inner mental and emotional craving. The Buddha promises that the doctrine he teaches for getting rid of the assumed self will bring about the disappearance of all defiling mental states, so that within us there will only be "purity and perfection of wisdom." Perhaps we can see that unpleasant mental states are always, and exclusively, concerned with ourselves. We tend to think they come to us from the outside. For instance, someone does something objectionable, not even to us but to another person, and we grow angry and upset. That is a defiling mental state. It may be quite true that the action was harmful, but our own negative reaction concerns us alone and is in any case useless. There are better ways of dealing with such a situation. We really have no excuses, though we may try to find them, and that, again, is the self making excuses for it-self!

The Buddha continues:

> Now, Poṭṭhapāda, you might think: "Perhaps these defiling mental states might disappear…and one might still be unhappy." That is not how it should be regarded. If defiling states disappear…nothing but happiness and delight develops, tranquillity, mindfulness and clear awareness—and that is a happy state.

Poṭṭhapāda has not practiced yet; he has no idea of what it would be like to lose his defiling states. The Buddha is forestalling a probable next question, telling him that if he thinks he might still be unhappy, he thinks wrongly. He is also saying that to be happy does not mean jumping with joy and feeling highly elated. When we are clearly aware, mindful and tranquil, we are in a state of equanimity, and that brings peaceful happiness. We must not confuse equanimity with indifference, though it is easy to do so. Indifference arises when we disassociate ourselves from what is happening, whereas equanimity is tranquility coupled with mindfulness and clear awareness.

We practice mindfulness when we meditate by keeping our awareness on the meditation subject. In everyday life we practice it to the best of our ability, by being mindful of whatever we are doing. When there is no longer any kind of defilement, mindfulness and clear awareness become our natural states of being. Clear awareness is another word for "insight-wisdom." It is not only directed inward, it also enables us to see others and their actions, with compassion and no trace of condemnation or dislike. When the mind is clear, it recognizes without rejection. The tranquility mentioned here is clearly part of equanimity. We practice it in meditation, and as we bring it into our daily lives, it gradually becomes our natural state.

Next, the Buddha says he teaches a doctrine for getting rid of the illusion of the gross acquired self and repeats the same for a mind-made acquired self and a formless acquired self.

He goes on:

Poṭṭhapāda, if others ask us: "What, friend, is this gross acquired self whose abandonment you preach...?" Being so asked, we should reply: "This *is* that gross acquired self for the getting rid of which we teach a doctrine...."

"This *is* that...self" means "this person is," pointing to ourselves. He repeats the question and its answer for both the mind-made and formless selves. All three, in other words, are illusions, for there is nothing in body, mind, or consciousness that can ever proclaim "me"; nothing within us that can say "I am the owner"; nothing that can say "I am the knower." It is simply a mental formation.

The Buddha asks:

"What do you think, Poṭṭhapāda, does not that statement turn out to be well-founded?"

"Certainly, Lord."

The Buddha explains:

"It is just as if a man were to build a staircase for a palace, which was below that palace. They might say to him: 'Well now, this staircase for a palace that you are building, do you know whether the palace will face east or west, or north or south, or whether it will be high, low or of medium height?' and he would say: 'This staircase is right under the palace.' Don't you think that man's statement would be well founded?"

"Certainly, Lord."

"In just the same way, Poṭṭhapāda, if others ask us 'What is the gross-acquired self...? What is this mind-made acquired self...? What is this formless acquired self...?' We reply: 'This *is* this [gross, mind-made, formless] acquired self for the getting rid of which we teach a doctrine whereby defiling mental states disappear and states tending to purification grow strong, and one gains and remains in the purity and perfection of wisdom here and now, having realized and attained it by one's own super-knowledge.' Don't you think that statement

is well-founded?"
"Certainly, Lord."

The Buddha is not asking Poṭṭhapāda to put all this into practice, he is only asking whether he thinks the doctrine is well-founded, and Poṭṭhapāda agrees that it is.

When we are able to let go of this acquired, or assumed, self, and the defiling mental states disappear, "one gains and remains in the purity and perfection of wisdom here and now." This is an important point. We not only gain wisdom, but we remain in it, because insight can never be lost. Calm and tranquil meditative states can disappear very easily, if we do not practice. Any insight we gain, however, changes our whole attitude, demeanor, and inner feeling. If really assimilated, an insight will always stay with us. That is why, after the meditative absorptions, or after any concentrated meditation, we should always ask ourselves: "What have I learned from this? What insight can I gain from this experience?"

What the Buddha is telling Poṭṭhapāda will not change him to any great extent yet. He is first of all gaining confidence in the teaching and will later start to practice. Change, however, requires the understood experience. After the mind has been calm to any extent whatsoever, we should investigate: "What does my dukkha consist of? Do I know how it arises?" or, "Where is this self I'm always concerned with, how can I find it?" or, "Can I see the impermanence of the flux and flow in everything that exists? Does this throw a different light on my presumed solidity?" Any one of these three characteristics—*anicca*, dukkha, anattā—can be examined. At a time of calm abiding, the mind is willing and able to be objective, and loses some of the duality within which we normally operate. With a calm mind we can let go of that to some extent and see things in a more realistic way.

All these steps tend toward purification and gain us insight-wisdom. The "perfection of wisdom here and now" is of course the final state of enlightenment, but purity is a prerequisite. If there is none within, it is very difficult for us to look at anything objectively. Meditation brings about purification, so we have that as our support system. Each insight should be nurtured and reinforced by bringing it up again and again and anchoring it in the mind. Then we will have access to it and be able to use it at all times.

# 1 2

# Which Is the Real Self?

Citta now enters into the conversation to pose a new question on the self. Here again, he and Poṭṭhapāda are not very different from us, for we too keep coming up with fresh ideas as we wrestle with this elusive subject of who we really are.

> At this, Citta, son of the elephant-trainer, said to the Lord: "Lord, whenever the gross acquired self is present, would it be wrong to assume the existence of the mind-made acquired self, or of the formless acquired self? Does only the gross acquired self truly exist then? And similarly with the mind-made acquired self and the formless acquired self?"

He is asking when only one of the acquired or assumed selves is present, what happens to the other two? In other words, he believes in the existence of all three. We can easily identify with his question. Let's say we are walking peacefully along and trip over a root on the path. We hurt our leg, which begins to bleed. We say to ourselves: "I've hurt my leg, I'd better do something about it immediately." So we go to a chemist and get an ointment to put on it. It hurts for a while, and we think: "Oh, my leg is really bad. I need something more for it." We get a massage, or acupuncture, or other medical treatment. At that time, the only self with which we are identified, the one which is of real importance to us, is the "gross acquired self," or the assumed bodily self. The translation of this sutta is scholarly, as it should be, and keeps as close as possible to the actual Pali words, but we sometimes need alternatives to make the meaning clearer.

We often assume we are this physical self. When we eat, for instance, we think, "I'm hungry; I want some food." After eating, we might say, "My stomach isn't quite full; I think I'll take a little more." We are concerned with "my" hunger, "my" body, "my" stomach. Citta is asking whether all three selves exist at such a moment, and the Buddha tells him:

> Citta, whenever the gross acquired self is present, we do not at that time speak of a mind-made acquired self, we do not speak of a formless acquired self. We speak only of a gross acquired self. Whenever the mind-made acquired self is present, we speak only of a mind-made acquired self, and whenever the formless acquired self is present, we speak only of a formless acquired self.

Obviously we are only aware of one self at a time. We assume ourselves to be the body, particularly, when there is a sensation of either pain or pleasure. The body very rarely has neutral moments, and as soon as it experiences any sensation a little more strongly, we identify with it. We know this from meditation practice. Immediately the body begins to feel uncomfortable, we become concerned with it, unless, of course, we have grown so concentrated that we are no longer aware of it. It does not take much to make us "be" the body. A simple cold, a bout of coughing, and immediately there is "me" having this problem.

There is also the mind-made acquired self. Let's say we have been very diligent in keeping the Buddhist precepts. We think: "That's good, I've been keeping the precepts." Keeping precepts is good, but at that moment, what are we identified with? Certainly the "I" that has been keeping the precepts and is now thinking about that. At other times the mind gets upset. It cannot meditate because it keeps thinking of something else, some obsessive thought or other, which comes up over and over again. We recognize the thinking mind and believe we are its owner. On the relative level, we are quite convinced it must be so. It is "me" who wants to meditate, and it is "me" who has been disturbed by these thoughts, so what else could it possibly be?

The mind-made self is of great importance because it is also the observer and our memory. For instance "I" remember the "me" of ten years ago. What is happening here is that one mind-made self is remembering another, so we end up with two. Of course we do not look at it that way. We say, "Well, somebody is remembering, so it must be me." We do not recognize that memory is simply memory, nothing more. Or we may be looking ahead, making useful plans for "me" in the future. There are still two "me's," although again we are not aware of it. All we know is that "I" am planning. We may also know that planning interferes with our meditation, but on the other hand, it is a pleasant pastime and takes us out of body-consciousness, where there may be aches and pains. Basically, the mind-made self is a mental formation that is saying, "That's me."

In fact, the mind-made self is always present. It starts up at the very moment of waking. If we are mindful enough, we can actually notice its arising. First there is nothing, and then all of a sudden the whole mind activity begins. "What time is it? What do I have to do today? Am I late? Is it cold?"—all taking place in the mind. The body has done nothing yet, except possibly open its eyes. All this mental activity is our support system for identifying with this special person, called "me." The "me" is also looking for an escape-hatch, a way out of dukkha, which creates all our restlessness, worry, planning, remembering; but it is not a way out at all—it leads to a dead end. These activities cannot take away any of our dukkha. They provide a momentary relief from it, which is why the whole world uses them. The underlying dukkha is always there, revealed by the niggling, restless movement of the mind, but when we make plans, we are not confronted with that for a moment. So we think, "What shall I do today? I'll have to go to work, but later I'll take a nice walk, or perhaps I'll invite friends to supper."

The mind-made self is the one we are most concerned with and the hardest to lose. We may say, "Yes, I know all that," but who is the knower? The teaching of Ramana Maharshi, an enlightened sage in southern India who died in the 1950s, was simply to ask the question: "Who am I?" Of course this is rather difficult to grasp, and we may need preparation, perhaps through other pathways or in other lifetimes, but that was his whole teaching. His disciple, Sri Nisargadatta Maharaj, who died in the 1980s, taught only "I am that," and to let go of everything else.

It does, eventually, all narrow down to that one essential point, and the Buddha is trying to show this in a way that is acceptable to his listener. If we want real happiness, the only way it can arise is by letting go of the one who is unhappy. It is not a question of trying to hold on to the one who is happy. Rather, when the unhappy one is relinquished, nothing else remains except the happiness of tranquility and pure awareness. We have endless opportunities to become aware of this self-seeking, mind-made self. "What am I going to do next year? Where shall I go? How can I arrange things to suit me?" The mind is constantly churning, searching, which cannot bring tranquility.

To see that this is so does not, of course, mean that we are rid of the mind-made self, but by recognizing it, we have taken a great step forward. As long as we are unaware, just following instinct and impulse, we are simply moving with the herd. Even though we may not notice that we have any inner dissatisfaction, the mind is nonetheless trying to get away from something, because otherwise it would stay exactly where it is, in the here and now. As soon as it tries to escape from the moment, it is attempting to avoid some kind of dukkha. Once we see that, we can begin to do something about it.

Another level of recognition arises, when we become aware that we have made up this self. This is not to say we can immediately get rid of it, but we are certainly hovering on the brink of being able to do so. Until then, it is important to notice our usual pattern of: "I'm thinking, I'm observing, I'm concentrating, I'm not concentrating," all concerned with "I am," or "I will be," or "I have been."

The Buddha now says:

> Citta, suppose they were to ask you: "Did you exist in the past or didn't you, will you exist in the future or won't you, do you exist now or don't you?" How would you answer?

Citta replies:

> Lord, if I were asked such a question, I would say: "I did exist in the past, I did not not exist; I shall exist in the future, I shall not not exist; I do exist now, I do not not exist." That, Lord, would be my answer."

Citta is quite convinced that his self has a present, a past, and a future; and so are we. There is nothing new in that; the only new thing, in his case, is that the Buddha is there to teach him otherwise.

Within that past, present, and future self, there are many false assumptions. First of all, we are making boundaries. The past self is the one we have in our memory. The present self is the one we rarely observe; we are aware that it is somewhere around, but we are hardly ever actually connected to it. The future self is the one on which we pin all our hopes; the one that is going to do wonderful things, be absolutely happy, become totally concentrated, and so on. We are quite certain that these three selves are all called "me." In fact, it is even more complicated than that. When we bring the past to mind, it is then the present. When we bring the future to mind, that also becomes the present. So what we are doing is not only putting boundaries around three separate selves, but we are also putting boundaries around time and splitting it into three parts as well. The result of all this is that we fail to live fully; because to live is to experience, and we can only experience now. All the rest is either memory or hope. By dividing both ourselves and time into three parts, we then find ourselves anxiously awaiting the future, or often regretfully thinking of the past. Happiness completely escapes us because, when we take that kind of stance, there is no room for it to arise. Pleasure does, but not happiness. Happiness or inner joy is always connected to tranquility, and a divided self in a divided time frame is not a tranquil state to be in. Since, however, everybody lives in this way, we are not even aware of how futile it is, or how false. We think life is like that, until we come into contact with the Buddha's teaching and see that it does not have to be that way, that there is another possibility. When, through mindfulness and meditation, we have become totally aware, if even only for one moment, we may have an inkling of what it is like to live in the present. The past is gone, the future has not arisen, only the moment exists, and it is eternal.

Citta, like the rest of us, is still trapped in the idea of a divided self existing in a divided time frame, and the Buddha is trying to get him to see this other reality, in a logical manner:

> But, Citta, if they asked: "The past acquired self that you had, is that your only true acquired self, and are the future and present ones false, or is the one you will have in the future the only true one, and are the past and present ones false? Or is your present acquired self the only true one, and are the past and future ones false?" how would you reply?

Citta says:

Lord, if they asked me these things, I would reply: "My past acquired self was at the time my only true one, the future and present ones were false. My future acquired self will then be the only true one, the past and present ones will be false. My present acquired self is now the only true one, the past and future ones are false." That is how I would reply.

So, having heard the Buddha's logical analysis, he sees that obviously he cannot have three selves. He decides that it must therefore have been "me" in the past, that it is "me" in the present, and will be "me" in the future. At least he has reduced it to only one self—whereas previously he had three of them. We too think of at least three selves, in fact most of us are sure of that.

If we look at our old photo albums, whom do we see there, apart from our friends? The past "me." That is why we take photos, so that the past will not escape us. "There I am," we say, and we are still seeing things as Citta did in the first instance. We think there are three of us. If we add the body and the mind, there are five of us. If on top of that we include the past in its movement through time—the distant past, the more recent past, yesterday—then we might have several hundred, should we have taken enough photos. In the end, we wind up with a self that is so fractured we cannot possibly point to it. If the Buddha were to ask us these same questions, we would answer as Citta did. We would quite agree we cannot be a hundred different selves, or even three, four, or five. Then we might say: "Well, the self is the one who is actually knowing now."

Citta is at just this point himself. He sees he cannot be three, so he must be the one that is happening now, and that one only. For those of us who have the ability to visualize, we can picture a whole host of "me's" disappearing into the past, and then a whole host of them going into the future. When we look at it this way, we can see the absurdity of it. It is impossible, but because we know nothing else; it is how we all live.

Mystics throughout the ages have always known something else, have always seen this fallacy. They knew we were making it all up, and we do this for one reason only: our craving for existence. If we were free from that craving, we would not bother to do so. The way to look at this is to see that the delusion of this assumed self creates the craving for existence, and vice versa—the craving for existence is the underlying cause for the delusion of the assumed self. The two work hand in hand; they co-exist and it is not possible to say "first this, then that."

Citta realizes now that he is "me, in this moment," and many of us would probably agree to that. He still has the formless acquired self to deal with. This is the self that we might call our consciousness. It is, in a way, our last resort. We are not the body, not the mind, so we must be the consciousness. One consciousness we are aware of is the one experienced in the jhānas. It is for this reason that the jhānas are mundane, not yet transcendental. They are not without "me." All the jhānas are of this nature; sometimes stronger, sometimes less so. In the first three absorptions the "me" aspect is very pronounced; less so in the fourth. It becomes strong again in the fifth, sixth, and seventh, but on a different level. Here it is an elevated consciousness, but still when "I" come out of them, "I" know what "I" experienced. In the eighth absorption, the "me" consciousness is very weak. In the jhānas, there is no body consciousness as we know it, otherwise we could not experience them properly. There are also no mind-made convolutions. When there is any kind of thought, the jhāna will stop. There is still, however, the elevated, concentrated consciousness, and we love to identify with it because it is most gratifying. It also seems quite an achievement; maybe something our friends can't do. Obviously, then, that consciousness has an owner, called "me."

There is another kind of consciousness, outside of meditation, and that is: "I am conscious of what is happening." We usually call this the observer, and it is the consciousness with which we are most intensely identified. If we agree to let go of the idea of being the body, and perhaps also agree that the four parts of the mind are not "me," nonetheless we can still find something called "me." It is our craving for existence, which is screaming: "I can't exist if there's no me." So we opt for the most refined "me," which is consciousness. This is what is referred to here as the formless acquired self. We might have intellectually given up the other two, but in reality we have not given up anything. If we were questioned, as Citta is, we might resort to the observer-consciousness, which we often feel to be separate from all other mind-states. There is sense consciousness, there is feeling, perception, mental formations—and then there is something that recognizes these. That this in itself is only a mental formation completely escapes us.

Citta has accepted that there is only one self, and that it is experienced in the moment. He agrees that in past moments it was "me," in the present moment it is "me," and in future moments it will be "me." Now the Buddha explains further and gives a simile:

> In just the same way, Citta, from the cow we get milk, from the milk curds, from the curds butter, from the butter ghee, and from the ghee, cream of ghee. And when there is milk we don't speak of curds, of butter, of ghee or of cream of ghee, we speak of milk; and when there are curds we don't speak of butter, of ghee or of cream of ghee, we speak of milk; when there are curds we don't speak of butter…when there is cream of ghee…we speak of cream of ghee.

The Buddha continues:

> So too whenever the gross acquired self is present, we do not speak of the mind-made or formless acquired self; whenever the mind-made acquired self is present, we do not speak of the gross or formless acquired self; whenever the formless acquired self is present, we do not speak of the gross acquired self or the mind-made acquired self, we speak of the formless acquired self. But, Citta, these are merely names, expressions, turns of speech, designations in common use in the world, which the Tathāgata uses without misapprehending them.

The Buddha is giving an important teaching here; showing Citta that, although this is how people commonly speak and what they believe, it is not true on an absolute level. It is simply how things appear to be, and he makes the point that when he, the Tathāgata, uses the same words, he does not misunderstand them. He speaks of all this on a relative level because he knows that neither Potthapāda nor Citta can go any further for the time being. The suttas often refer to the Buddha's ability to teach on a level appropriate to his listener.

Two truths, the Buddha, best of all who speak, declared;
conventional and ultimate, no third can be.
Terms agreed are true by usage of the world.
Words of ultimate significance are true in terms of dhammas.
Thus the Lord, a teacher, he who's skilled in this world's
speech, can use it and not lie.[4]

Our conventional way of speaking is not a lie, because it is how we all see things and understand each other. There are, however, other ways of understanding, in terms of ultimate significance, of the Dhamma and of dhammas. When written with a small *d* and an *s* at the end, the word means "phenomena," "everything that exists." Dhamma with a capital D and no final s is "the teaching of the Buddha," or "truth," or "law of nature."

The Buddha is quite content if Citta understands the idea that there can only be a momentary self. He gives him the simile of the milk and ghee to underline how one thing arises from another, even though we only see the one that is confronting us at the moment. He leaves it at that, not attempting to show Citta how, on an absolute level, this too is wrong. He knows both Citta and Poṭṭhapāda must first tread the practice path. If they fail to do so, all they have been told will remain at an intellectual level, and they will continue to find new arguments that, in the end, lead them nowhere. To argue about what is self and what is not self, why there is not a self, why we cannot have the one we like, rather than the one we don't like, and so on, does not lead to insight. Wanting a self that we can like is connected to the idea of a soul, and this too is another self-view. We see the soul as the "good" self, which is not part of the "me" I do not like. We all fall into these traps; people are the same everywhere.

Now comes a traditional explanation, which is found at the end of almost every sutta, because the suttas were recited for about two hundred and fifty years before being committed to writing, and the recitation had to stay exactly the same so that no errors crept in:

And at these words Poṭṭhapāda the wanderer said to the Lord: "Excellent, Lord, excellent! It is as if someone were to set up what had been knocked down, or to point out the way to one who had got lost, or to bring an oil-lamp into a dark place, so that those with eyes could see what was there. Just so the Blessed Lord has expounded the Dhamma in various ways. Lord, I go for refuge to the Lord, the Dhamma and the Sangha. May the Lord accept me as a lay-follower who has taken refuge in him from this day forth as long as life shall last!"

Here Potthapāda shows he is convinced of the Buddha's teaching, wants to be a lay-follower, and takes refuge in the Buddha, the Dhamma, and the Sangha. Taking refuge is a way of expressing commitment to the practice, love and devotion to the teaching, and is also a way of finding a mental/emotional shelter, which can result in great happiness. It is done in the same way to this day, only Potthapāda was able go to the Buddha himself for refuge. We, nowadays, go to the enlightenment principle embodied in the Buddha, who was a historical figure, a human being just like ourselves, and became fully enlightened. That same principle exists in all of us. To take refuge in the Buddha means to recognize that fact with devotion, love, and gratitude. We recognize the Dhamma, the teaching, as our greatest support for happiness; and also the Sangha, those who became enlightened by following the Buddha's teaching and have propagated the Dhamma for over two thousand five hundred years, so that it is still available to us today. When we go for refuge to these three, we feel gratitude, devotion, and commitment, and if we follow the guidelines and actually understand their truth, then we have protection from the dangers of the world and from our own instincts. Taking refuge can give an underlying sense of steadfastness and may help us to stay with our practice. Most people find it difficult to persevere; they may sometimes take time out from their worldly duties to practice, but it remains intermittent.

It can be helpful to remember that there is something far greater than ourselves. To be aware of this brings a sense of humility. This is not an inferiority complex; they are two entirely different emotions. To feel inferior implies "I am less than you are," whereas a sense of humility is the awareness that we are not quite as important as we thought we were. It is a step toward the realization of "non-self." As long as "I" am important, there is no way "I" can let go of this mental formation of self. Humility is actually part of the path; it means seeing ourselves in the right light. Not blaming ourselves, not feeling unworthy; true humility is recognizing we are still enmeshed in the follies of the world. Perhaps we are no longer so caught up in unskillful physical behavior, but even foolish mental activity is enough. As long as we are still involved in all this, we do not have the clarity and perfection we can see in the Buddha's teaching. When we recognize the total purity and humility of the Buddha's own life, we may be inspired to follow that example.

This is what Poṭṭhapāda is now doing. He takes refuge "as long as life shall last." When we take refuge in the Buddha, the Dhamma, and the Sangha, we do not do it halfheartedly, or as a temporary measure. We do it in order to live with it and practice accordingly.

Citta, too, has something to say. First he repeats Poṭṭhapāda's words:

> Excellent, Lord, excellent! It is as if someone were to set up what had been knocked down or to point out the way to one who had got lost, or to bring an oil-lamp into a dark place, so that those with eyes could see what was there. Just so the Blessed Lord has expounded the Dhamma in various ways. Lord, I go for refuge to the Lord, the Dhamma and the Sangha.

He then adds:

> May I, Lord, receive the going-forth at the Lord's hands, may I receive ordination.

He is asking to be a *bhikkhu*, "a monk." At that time, this was a simple matter; the Buddha would just say, "Come, bhikkhu." Nowadays it is an elaborate ritual, involving the taking of many precepts. In the early days of the Buddha's ministry, there were no rules for the monks to keep, for none of them misbehaved. But as time went on and more and more people joined the Sangha, this changed, and every time something went wrong, the Buddha made a new rule. At one stage there were 75, then 115, and then 150. We finally wound up with 227. If the Buddha were alive today, he would probably have to add a few more.

Some of those rules are no longer relevant and have no application to the world as we know it today. We cannot transfer the India of two thousand five hundred years ago to the Western civilization of the twentieth century. The main rules have, of course, retained their validity. The minor ones cannot really be broken because they no longer apply. For instance, the Buddha made rules to cover almost every possibility, even how to go to the toilet, which in those days could have resulted in harming various plants. The elaborate ordination rituals began when it became impossible for the Buddha to do everything himself. He could no longer look after each member of the Sangha personally, and so he allowed senior monks to ordain new ones. Rituals were laid down that had to be followed, and these are very similar to those we perform to this day.

> And Citta, son of the elephant-trainer, received the going-forth at the Lord's hands, and the ordination.

Going forth means to go from the home life to one that is homeless. This does not imply having no roof over our heads, but rather that we no longer live a family life. At one time the monks and nuns did not in fact have anywhere to live, as there were no monasteries. Later these were built, and they had huts, or *kuṭīs*. The homeless life means owning nothing at all, neither a kuṭī or anything else.

> And the newly ordained Venerable Citta, alone, secluded, unwearying, zealous and resolute, in a short time attained to that, for the sake of which young men of good birth go forth from the household life into homelessness, that unexcelled culmination of the holy life, having realized it here and now by his own super-knowledge and dwelt therein, knowing: "Birth is destroyed, the holy life has been lived, what had to be done has been done, there is nothing further here."

"Birth is destroyed, the holy life has been lived." When the practice reaches its culmination, there is no longer the feeling of a person, or an entity, within the phenomena of mind and body. If we have not experienced this, we cannot really know what it is like. We may infer, however, that if there is no longer a "me" sitting inside, then there is nobody to get worried, nobody who needs to plan, or remember, or feel insecure. There is simply mind and body doing whatever needs to be done. This is what the Buddha did for the forty-five years of his ministry. "Birth is destroyed," because birth comes about through craving for existence, which can only be present if there is someone there to experience it. When there is no longer that someone, there is no craving, and thus no rebirth. As we heard in the story of Vacchagotta, when no new fuel is put on the fire, it goes out. The sutta continues:

> And the venerable Citta, son of the elephant-trainer, became another of the Arahants.

To be an elephant trainer, incidentally, was a highly regarded and well-paid profession. In Sri Lanka a "mahout" is, to this day, an important person. However, although the suttas often refer, as here, to "young men of good birth," this does not mean riches, or high caste. The Buddha was not class conscious; he took anyone into the Sangha, such as a street cleaner or a barber, which were two of the lowest castes in those days. He said inner development was all that mattered and was utterly opposed to the idea of class distinction. When the text refers to "good birth," we can assume that what is meant is that the young man came from a family that cared for its children and household in an appropriate manner.

As the sutta tells us, the goal for going forth from the household life into the homeless life is to become an arahant. This is "that unexcelled culmination of the holy life" that Citta realizes "here and now by his own super-knowledge." There is no further mention of Poṭṭhapāda, the main protagonist in the sutta. All we are told is that he went for refuge. We can only hope that he, too, started practicing. Citta, who came into the story at the very end, is the one who committed himself fully. The above conclusion of the sutta is also the traditional ending of any sutta, when somebody has asked for ordination; the words are always exactly the same.

This sutta in its totality allows us an insight into how hard it is for people to realize they are thinking in the wrong way, even if the Buddha himself is giving them the teaching. The sense of self is deeply ingrained in most of us, and we cling fast to our viewpoints; the three selves of body, mind, and consciousness; the selves of past, present, and future. Those of us who like to analyze and reason it all out do not realize that this line of thought leads nowhere. There are some, however, who do not even make such an attempt, for they can see immediately that it brings no benefit or happiness. Their only concern is to let go.

Although the subtitle of this sutta is "States of Consciousness," it really addresses the consciousness of self.

# Path and Fruition:
# The Goal of the Practice

The sutta we have studied has taken us all the way from the beginning to the end of practice, explaining to us what needs to be done. At this point it is appropriate to look at the final result of following these guidelines, which go from our moral conduct, through concentration, to insight-wisdom. The insight that eventually arises is that we look at our self-illusion and recognize it for what it is.

We have seen in the sutta that we cannot in fact be the multiple selves we experience and call "I." Each is there for a moment, then disappears, and a new one arises. There is a self that is concerned solely with the body, and at that time it seems to be "I," then up pops another, which is concerned with mental formations, the mind; then that too disappears as our consciousness latches onto something else. None of these selves is stable and reliable; nor are our past, present, and future selves anything solid. They all disappear; a moment ago we had one self, now we have another. On top of that, we can look at all our previous selves and ask where, in the present, are they to be found? This is particularly telling if we remember ourselves doing something, which we would now never do. Which of those two do we call the real "me"? We can never take hold of the self; it is always moving. We might compare it to a meandering brook. If we want to seize hold of that brook, and we put our hand into the water to try to grab it, nothing stays within our grasp. The brook just moves on; if it did not, it would no longer be a brook, but a stagnant pool.

To come to the point in our practice where we begin to see our self-illusion for what it is, we may need different approaches. Some people recognize it through awareness of dukkha; they grow so heartily tired of their own suffering that they are able to let go every time they experience it. Others see the impermanence of self, which has just been mentioned. Some approach it by an analysis of what they consider self to be and come to recognize that their theory is based on an unknown quantity, and therefore can never result in a sound equation. Some use all three. These are the three characteristics of being: anicca, dukkha, and anattā; "impermanence," "unsatisfactoriness," and "corelessness," which constitute the essence of any insight.

On the path of practice it is essential to keep these three in mind, for in worldly life everything is made to look as if it were permanent and would really bring satisfaction, and as if each person was a separate, definable entity. The worldly standpoint is not at all conducive to practice, and we have to make a sustained effort to remember the three characteristics, to check them out against all we experience through our senses, including what we think. If we forget to do this, we are forgetting the spiritual path. The path is not simply a question of meditation, though that is of course an essential ingredient, for without it the mind refuses to change its direction. But outside of meditation we should also remember what we are trying to do and notice how we go about it. Are we pointing our efforts in the right direction? Are we trying to get out of dukkha by seeing the truth, or are we trying to get out of it by looking for more sukha? Which way do we incline? If we want to see the truth, we must look for it as often and as diligently as we possibly can. There is a veil, or a fog, or sometimes even a brick wall, surrounding the mind of the ordinary person. We may be a meditator, but in all likelihood we are still a worldling, a *puthujjana*, someone who has not yet experienced "path and fruit." They are the result of diligent practice, and for this reason it seems appropriate to give some description of them here.

A "path-moment" is known as *magga*, and the "moment of fruition" that follows it is known as *phala*. Together they are called *magga-phala* and are our aim on this path. When they occur, a great and lasting change takes place in the meditator. They become an *Ariyā*, a noble one and, it is said, now belong to the lineage of true followers of the Buddha.

How do we come to a path-moment? It can never happen unless we really understand all that has been said previously concerning the self-illusion. This means understanding it from the ground up, not as a possibility but as a reality, about which we do not have the slightest trace of doubt. We must be absolutely convinced that all we think of as "self" is simply an idea. That everyone else has the same idea makes no difference. We can ask ourselves: "Are these people happy and contented? Or is their idea of 'self' in fact the cause of their difficulties?" When we are completely convinced and are totally willing to give up our self-illusion, there comes a moment when we can make the attempt to do so. Giving it up is not so easily done as said, but at least it can be explained.

After any of the jhānas is the right moment to try. The first jhāna is not particularly suitable, although the Buddha says it can be done after any one of them. The third, fourth, fifth, sixth, and seventh are all most useful because the mind is particularly at ease and clear of the hindrances. When these are present, it is impossible for us to see truth because we are obstructed by the hindrances. But when we come out of a jhāna, during which they have been laid aside, the mind is tranquil and translucent, and it becomes possible at that time to recognize other dimensions.

We can, in fact, make the attempt after any concentrated meditation; but unless the concentration has been long and steady enough, the hindrances will still be present. It is essential to have an unperturbed mind.

At this time we can once more review the way we think of the self, using all the understanding we have gained of its being nothing but an illusion. Then we ascertain whether we are willing to give up this conglomeration of feeling and knowing, the seeming certainty that "this is me." When the mind says, without hesitation: "Yes, I want to give that up because I realize it is the cause of dukkha; it is nothing but an ever-moving flux and flow, and selfhood has no basis in reality," and affirms that this is really the purpose of our practice. Then we can quite intentionally direct the mind toward what is called the still-point. This is a mental formation where nothing at all is happening. The mind might comply with our intention. There must be no hindrances present, no hint of doubt such as "Perhaps this is 'me' trying to get something out of this." That would not work. But if the mind is free and tranquil enough, it will direct itself toward that point where absolutely nothing is happening. At such a time, there is no experiencer, and because of this, we cannot describe the path-moment other than that it is a moment of nothing, "standing still." It is quite different from the seventh jhāna, which is the base of nothingness, no-thingness. In the jhāna there is an experiencer, who knows exactly what has happened, namely that there is not a single solid building block in the whole of existence. But here is one single mind-moment where everything seems to stop.

Immediately following it, however, comes the moment of fruition, in which certain characteristics will always be present. Because of this, it is easy for a teacher to verify, when a meditator recounts his or her experience, whether it really happened, or whether the meditator was close to it but not yet quite there, or whether it was just a case of wishful thinking. Not all the characteristics will be present each time for everyone, but certain ones will always be repeated. The moment of fruition can be blissful, it can be joyful. It may be neither, but it is always, and invariably, a moment of total relief. It is as if we had let go of an enormous burden. The feeling of relief is so pronounced it may even bring tears to our eyes. They are not tears of sadness, but of release from stress. The feeling of bliss may come later, for although the moment of fruition happens immediately after the path-moment, it is not confined to that instant. We may experience bliss the next day, as we re-experience the feeling of complete relief.

Something else is common to all experiences of path and fruition; the certain knowledge that just for a moment nobody was there, and that this is the deepest truth we have ever known. This certainty is particularly marked in the first moment of fruition, and obviously so, for never before will we have experienced anything like it. For one single mind-moment the "person" was totally eliminated.

We know how quick a mind-moment is. The knowing and the relief take two, at the most three, moments. The relief, the release, the tears can last and perhaps turn into bliss later on, if it does not happen straightaway. The knowing arises immediately and when it does, we realize what we have practiced for. There may even be a feeling of having actually lost weight, as if the body had become much lighter. In fact it is the mind which has lightened, but the mind greatly influences the body.

There is a very nice analogy in the *Visuddhimagga* (*Path of Purification*), a thick volume of commentary on the Buddha's teaching, written by a monk called Buddhaghosa, who lived in Sri Lanka in the fifth century. It can be difficult to read, for it is so minutely detailed, but as a reference book it is very useful and contains many analogies. This one is particularly apt.

He describes a river, where the near bank represents worldly life and the other bank the experience of Nibbāna. On the near bank there is a huge tree, and one of its branches, with a rope attached, overhangs the river. The branch depicts our usual way of thinking about ourselves, our materiality. This still exists on the spiritual path, for whenever we think "I" am doing it, that too is materiality. The rope, tied to the branch, represents our clinging to the idea of selfhood. We catch hold of the rope and with the momentum of practice, while still holding on, we swing across the river. If, at the appropriate moment, we are willing and able to let go of our selfhood, we release our grasp and let ourselves fall on the opposite bank.

Of course none of this imagery need go on in our minds; it is only an analogy, but can be helpful. When we fall onto the far bank of the river, we feel unsteady at first. We are in a new, unknown situation and have to find our feet. It is not uncommon, after a path-moment, to have a jittery feeling, as if something momentous, but hard to describe, had happened. It is neither pleasant nor unpleasant, it is simply a reaction, depicted here as falling down on the other bank and having to find a foothold. Some people steady themselves immediately, others after a day or so, yet others may need the help of a teacher. Then we can happily enjoy the other side of the river. We get used to being a different person. We look exactly as we did before, nobody, except perhaps our teacher, would know anything, but inside we feel totally changed.

We have, at that time, automatically let go of the first three of ten fetters, which the Buddha described as our chains to *saṃsāra*—the round of rebirths. The ten fetters are: (1) wrong view of self; (2) belief in rites and rituals; (3) skeptical doubt; (4) greed; (5) hate; (6) craving for fine-material existence; (7) craving for formless existence; (8) conceit; (9) restlessness; and (10) ignorance. It is these that bind us to the conditioned state. The Buddha actually named his little son "Rahula," which means "the fetter."

The first and foremost fetter to be lost, which takes pride of place, is that we change from wrong view to right view. We will never again believe that there is a person sitting inside us; that a man or a woman looks out through our eyes, hears through our ears, thinks through our mind, wishes through our desires. We will not believe it because we have had absolute proof, on which we can rely that this is a mistaken and wrong view. But this right view only arises for those who have had the first path-moment, when they direct their mind to it. Although the inner feeling changes dramatically, it does not change to the point of no longer having any sense of a "me" within. That only comes later. However, whenever we put our mind to the question "Who am I?" we now know without a shadow of a doubt that we are the phenomena of mind and body. We know we have arisen through craving, that all craving is dukkha, that the idea of a "me" is the cause of all problems, and that the whole world suffers from it. The wrong view of self can never arise again, but the feeling of being a person, as we walk around and talk to people, is still there. What is necessary after that first step, is to reinforce this right view of self by bringing it into consciousness as often as we possibly can. It is particularly important to do so when we are confronted with something we do not like, for that is when the ego starts playing up. If, at that time, we do not remember our deepest insight, we may fall into the trap of negative reaction, for we have only taken a very first step; hate and greed have not yet been touched. The ability to bring up the right view as often as we can is an essential support.

A person who has accomplished this first step is known as a stream-enterer, which means someone who has entered the stream leading to Nibbāna. This is an irreversible step. In the scriptures it is said that such a person will have a maximum of seven more lifetimes and can even reach Nibbāna in this present life. Usually, anyone who has become a stream-enterer will be extremely aware of the difficulties they face, knowing that hate and greed are still present, and will be determined to go ahead and finish with all that. As a result, the practice gains momentum.

The stream-enterer has also lost two other fetters. One is skeptical doubt, which is always very damaging to practice. It prevents us from doing what needs to be done; for instead, we allow the mind to go into all kinds of speculation about how things might be done differently; we waste a great deal of mental energy and time on this and may even get to the point where we stop practicing altogether. After that first experience of path and fruition, however, there is no longer any possibility of doubting the Buddha's teaching. All skepticism concerning the Buddha, the Dhamma, and the Sangha disappears completely. He said there was "nobody there," and we have now seen the truth of this for ourselves. The beauty and ease of mind connected with this experience are far greater than in any of the meditative absorptions. There is full confidence, full devotion, full gratitude, and strong determination. The scriptures say that when the Buddha sat under the Bodhi Tree he experienced all four path and fruition moments—(1) stream-enterer; (2) once-returner; (3) non-returner; and

(4) arahant—in one single meditation. For us, it is a tremendous achievement to get to the first of them. People who do so, however, are rarely contented to leave it at that, and this is as it should be, for the mind can certainly go further. Another doubt that is eliminated is doubt in our own ability, for we now know we belong to those who can rise above ordinary consciousness, so that we are imbued with self-confidence.

Self-confidence is not a feeling of superiority, which is usually followed by a feeling of inferiority. Self-confidence is a feeling of inner strength, which does not have to prove anything, for there is nothing to prove, nowhere to go, nobody there. This inner certainty helps our practice, as does the devotion for and confidence in the Buddha, the Dhamma, and the Sangha—the Three Jewels.

The third fetter lost at the time of stream-entry is the belief in rites and rituals. All over the world there are strongly held views that particular rites and rituals are actually capable of purifying us, to the point where they even free us from all our dukkha. This belief was widespread in India in the Buddha's time, as it is today, though he himself always denied that rites and rituals have any such power. This false belief completely disappears, for we have experienced for ourselves that the first path-moment had absolutely nothing to do with such things but comes from clarity of mind and a willingness to totally let go. This does not mean we can no longer perform rituals, but we no longer want to give too much time and energy to them and tend to reduce them to a minimum. There are, however, certain aspects of ritual, for instance chanting and paying homage to the qualities of the Buddha—Dhamma-Sangha, which do have a purifying effect, if they are done mindfully rather than mechanically. This is also true of mantras, for if we repeat the words with full attention and devotion, there can be no negativities in the mind at that time. If it is done mechanically, we can say the words and simultaneously be full of bad feelings.

When we become stream-enterers, our minds have grown more refined than they were before, and because of this we will be far more conscious of greed and hate, and find them much more troublesome when they arise. What previously would hardly have bothered us, what we might have seen as a slight mishap, now becomes a real disturbance. This, in fact, is a great spur to our practice. It is not a superficial knowing that we should behave well, but rather a need for inner purity at all times.

In order to go from the first path-moment to the second, the mind has to be ripe. It does not usually happen quickly; most people need time, especially if they live in the world. In its whole attitude, customs, and social conduct, the world is against such things. It does not support this kind of practice, and so we have to be very strong within ourselves.

To take the next step, there are two things we should bring to mind over and over again; right view of "self" and, particularly, the remembrance of the moment of fruition. This will not have such an impact as when it first occurred but will certainly bring back the feeling of relief and joy. Both are needed and must be brought up as often as possible.

It is also very helpful to review the hindrances, seeing which are still strong and which have abated. Skeptical doubt, the fifth, should have gone. The first two, desire for sensual gratification and ill-will, are manifestations of greed and hate. We should also investigate the third and fourth: sloth and torpor; and restlessness and worry. It is only through constant enquiry and awareness that we can lessen their hold on us. "Which hindrance is strongest in me now? How does it manifest?" Of course everyone, at whatever point they may be on the path, should investigate in this way. It needs to be done with the understanding that these hindrances exist in all of us and can only be minimized through the practice of substitution. We will be far less inclined to blame others if we are aware of our own lack of purity.

For stream-enterers, this objective honesty is much easier, for they know without a shadow of a doubt that they are simply looking at mind and body phenomena. There is no "self" sitting inside who can be blamed for having these hindrances. Those of us who have not experienced Stream-entry will have a harder time of it, because we do not really like to know our negative qualities.

It is also said that a stream-enterer can no longer break any of the five precepts (to refrain from: killing living beings; taking what is not freely given; sexual misconduct; lying and wrong speech;and the use of alcohol and mind-altering drugs). We should check this out and see whether we are actually living with these precepts to the point where they have become, not a burden, but simply a natural lifestyle.

These are all examples of what is called "review-knowledge," especially useful after any of the jhānas. At that time, when the mind is pure and translucent, we bring up the feeling of the moment of fruition and then review our whole understanding of the fallacy of selfhood. We need to internalize this fallacy many times with the recognition that there is no longer any wish to cherish it. It is not that we blame the self, or want to alter it, but rather that we recognize it as something we have conjured up. We need to review everything that brought us to this understanding, all the reasons we can find. Having reviewed our understanding and feeling, we then see whether the mind is willing and able to let go of the slightest clinging to anything that constitutes "me." Are we willing to dissolve this person completely? Not with any reservation, any thought that "I" can come right back afterward, because that, of course, would be counterproductive. As before, we let the mind reach for the still-point. We may find that, although we make the attempt several, even many times, the mind will not go along. If so, we need to investigate what it is we are clinging to. We may come up with many things, but in the last analysis, we do not want to let go of the one who knows and is experiencing.

The momentum of practice may, in the first instance, have taken us across the river. In order to repeat that, however, we have to let go completely of everything that has to do with "self." If there is an underlying clinging to any aspect whatsoever of human life—sensual desire, sexual desire, whatever it may be—we cannot take the next step. We must be determined to work on this. "To what am I so attached that I can't let go of it?" As we investigate this, we may be able to see that, if we are clinging to other people, it makes us dependent and fearful. A loved one can disappear at any moment, and our attachment creates nothing but dukkha. Or if we are clinging to a desire, we can see that any gratification brings only momentary fulfillment. All too soon we feel as empty as we did before, and the desire has to be satisfied again and again. These are all ways and means of acknowledging our attachments, because we really want to know the truth. Naturally, there are those of us who do not want to reach into such depths, and that is perfectly all right. But if we are solidly on the path, these are steps to be taken, insights to be realized.

Anyone who has been able to take the second step becomes a once-returner, which means they only have to come back to this world one more time. Since these steps are irreversible, both stream-enterer and once-returner will be reborn with their experience intact. Because of this they can be very helpful to others, for they will be born with the necessary true understanding and can therefore teach it to us.

When this second step is taken, greed and hate are halved. They are not eliminated, but hate becomes irritation, greed becomes preference. The person's mind is never again shaken by real hate and greed, for irritation and preference cannot disturb the mind to the same extent. Irritation has a shorter time span than hate, and both irritation and preference are much milder passions than hate and greed. Once again, however, review knowledge, which the once-returner continues to use, will show that both still create dukkha.

A once-returner can expect to have a path-moment that is similar to, but not identical with, the previous one, and that in any case defies description, followed by a similar, but not identical fruit-moment. The jittery feeling is, in most instances, no longer apparent. Utter relief arises, but usually no tears. It can be extremely blissful, though this need not happen immediately. Again the mind has touched upon a moment of nothingness, which is an actual experience. It is not that bodies, trees, houses, cars, roads, bushes, and mountains do not exist. On the relative level they do. But on an absolute level they are particles of energy that come together and fall apart. They come together in certain forms and create phenomena. The moment of nothing is the experience of that one moment when everything has fallen apart and has not yet arisen again.

However, preceding the path- and fruition-moments, we have to gain a number of insights. The first is that mind and body are two, dependent on each other but not identical. The second is that everything that arises must, of its nature, cease. The third is dissolution, that everything falls apart; and when we see this without having had a path-moment, it can create a great deal of fear. If this happens, it is very important to talk to a teacher and get new courage. We need to know that it is quite all right because fear is a step on the insight path. The understanding of cause and effect also lies within those insight moments. As we have seen in this sutta, there is the gross material body, made up of the four elements and nourished by material food. They are the causes, the body is the effect. We must take note of that.

Having come, on our insight path, to the fear and having been able to leave it behind, the urgency of practice and the desire for liberation arise. Then, disenchantment and dispassion enable us to enter into a path-moment where we experience the reality of things as they are. The moment of fruition that follows has such impact that it can never be questioned. Each moment of fruition is somewhat stronger than the one before, and as a consequence the preceding ones usually fade a little in the memory. It is always the latest one, which we remember most, and that is as it should be, for it is the one that brings the greatest happiness and relief.

The fact that very few people experience path-moments should not surprise us. Most of the world is motivated by, and solely concerned with, hate and greed, and it takes two path-moments, a lot of hard work, and a great deal of meditation before we even get to the point where these fetters are lessened.

Having arrived at this stage, there are then two further steps to be taken, and they are by far the most difficult. We have to give ourselves up so completely that hate and greed can be totally eliminated. After another path-moment with the result of all five so-called "lower" fetters gone, a person then becomes a non-returner, meaning that they will never again return to the human realm. The path is never easy, and even for the non-returner there are still the five subtle, or higher, fetters to work on. Only an arahant, in whom the notion of "self" has been completely eradicated, loses these. Should a non-returner die before becoming an arahant, they will be reborn in one of the divine, or Brahmā realms. This may sound very pleasant, but in fact that is exactly one of the five fetters. The reason the non-returner has not become an arahant is the latent desire for rebirth in one of these formless, or fine-material, realms.

In the non-returner, the fetters of ignorance and conceit, through which these desires arise, are both still present. Ignorance simply means there is the very faintest lingering remnant of a "me." Conceit has nothing to do with being a conceited person; it means there is a "conceiving" of a self. Because of these two, the fetter of restlessness will also be there. Of course, it bears no comparison to that worldly unrest that drives people from one place or thing to another in search of happiness. But for the non-returner, because that faint "me" experience has not yet been lost, there will still be a niggling feeling of not being totally removed from all dukkha. At this point in the practice, recognition of what is happening within is far more subtle than ever before. The gross hindrances are gone, and even though the same word is used, the restlessness experienced by the non-returner is a much more refined one. It is instantly recognized and can immediately be dropped. It indicates, however, to that person that there is still something to be done.

For a once-returner who wants to become a non-returner, the guidelines are the same as before. They review the fetters and make very certain that the first three are gone and that hate and greed have greatly lessened. It is not a question of suppressing anything, but simply of noticing what is left. As a once-returner, we still experience an "I," to a far greater extent than a non-returner does. When we put our mind to it, and check it out, we know that nobody is there. At other times, in our ordinary, everyday life, we can usually feel as if there is a "somebody" talking and responding. This is because, to some degree, we still experience hate and greed. So, we summon up right view. We bring up the latest fruit-moment, and review all our understanding of the fallacy of selfhood. This understanding has to be exhaustive and at the deepest level, for to become a non-returner is an extreme step for anyone. The understanding must not only be reviewed from an intellectual standpoint, it must be felt, and complete commitment and dedication to getting rid of anything that still clings to the worldly life must be aroused. Particularly, anything in mind or body that has the slightest connotation of a "me." The determination must be extremely strong. Then comes, as before, the path-moment when the mind goes to the still-point, where nothing is happening. This time the path-moment may be a little different, for the mind has already become used to it, having experienced two such moments. It may be very short, and the moment of fruition that follows, may be nothing more than a recognition. No tears, no excitement, just complete knowing and clarity, accompanied by relief, a feeling of "Well, that's finally done." It does not have the same impact as before but is rather a feeling of satisfaction that the practice has borne fruit. At the same time the mind knows very well that there are still some fetters to be abandoned.

The non-returner has to review the remaining fetters and find out whether there is any wish for rebirth in the higher realms. This could manifest as a wish for everything to be pleasant and agreeable; a wish not to be confronted by anything containing dukkha. Of course this is also a very human attitude, but for the non-returner it is more. It becomes a kind of inner drive, for the fine-material and formless realms are said to consist of nothing but *sukha*, happiness. The feeling can be quite strong, and has to be recognized. The subtle remainder of self has to be seen for what it is. The Buddha warned against this desire to be reborn in higher realms because, once there, we stay for countless eons. This is why gods imagine themselves to be eternal. In the human realm, we have the constant incentive of dukkha to spur us on, but for the non-returner, once in those Brahma realms, experiencing no dukkha, it would be very hard to take the last step. This is why the Buddha said such a desire is detrimental to our practice.

The non-returner will be encouraged to go a step further, not only because it is the last thing that needs to be done, but particularly because they can feel that this remaining faint restlessness is still dukkha; this last little bit of desire, even if it is a desire for higher realms, is still painful; this subtle, lingering sense of selfhood is still unsatisfactory.

Taking the final step amounts to following the same guidelines as before. There is perhaps one slight difference, in that the mind resolves, once and for all, that this mind-and-body person is utterly willing to disappear. There is nothing more to hold us here, nothing of importance, nothing that needs to be done. The path-moment, as always, is indescribable—the technical term for it is "non-occurrence." Because of this total willingness to disappear, the fruit-moment contains that feeling. This may sound alarming; the Buddha himself says that for the worldling who has not experienced it, this could well seem a terrible thing. In fact, it is wonderful, for that disappearance creates enormous bliss. The experience is hard to describe; perhaps it best compares to falling into the depths of a cloud and disappearing in it. Afterward, nothing that happens in the world can ever again have the same impact. It is all taking place, but it is comparable to playing games with a child. We are very nice to that child, get along with it well. If it plays with building blocks, we show an interest, help it build a little tower or castle. But do we take the game seriously? If someone accidentally stepped on the tower or castle, the child might scream, but we would not. Of course we help people build castles, if the opportunity arises; we may even try to help them to see that these castles are not really worth building; but none of it is serious. It is just happening. This analogy, I think, makes it quite clear what the result is, and the person who has taken this step, who has attained complete obliteration of selfhood, is able to get back to that utter bliss of disappearance any time they wish.

It is said in the scriptures that after his attainment of Nibbāna, the Buddha sat in the bliss of Nibbāna for a week and then decided he would show others the way. This total disappearance of the feeling of "self" is the culmination of the path. As it says in the scriptures, it is for this that young men from good families leave their homes for the homeless life, do the work, and realize at the end that all that needed to be done has been accomplished. There is nothing further to come.

# Loving-Kindness Meditations

## 1. Joy and Love: *A Beautiful Inner Vision*

In order to start the meditation please put the attention on the breath for just a few moments.

See the night sky in your own heart with the beautiful moon and many twinkling stars, all shining and bright, beautiful to see, lovely to experience, creating an inner vision that brings joy and happiness to your heart. Look at that inner vision of shining lights and be joyful with that experience and let the warmth of your love embrace that beautiful vision within, which is yours to create and yours to see and experience. Enjoy it, and love it, and feel the joy and the warmth of love.

Now think of the person sitting nearest you, having an equally beautiful vision in his or her heart and share your joy and love with that person, enjoying and loving your togetherness.

Think of your parents, whether they are still alive or not, and share your love and joy with them. As you see your own beautiful inner vision of light, you realize that they, too, have such an inner vision, and you share your joy and love of that beauty with them.

Think of those people who are nearest and dearest to you, and share your joy of the beauty within and the warmth of your love with them. Let them take part, let them know, that you want to give them a gift.

Think of all your good friends and share the beauty of your inner vision, your joy and your love of it, with each one of your friends. Let them feel that you are giving them the gift of your heart.

Think of those people who are part of your daily life, whoever comes to mind. Share the beauty of the vision within you, your joy in it and your love for it with them. Give them that as a gift from you. Let them feel that you are near to them.

Think of a difficult person and share your own beautiful inner vision, your joy and the warmth of your love for that inner vision with that person; forgiving and forgetting all difficulties, creating togetherness.

Let the joy and the love for the beauty within you reach out to as many people as you can think of. Let it be like a golden stream coming from your heart, so that this joy and love can be shared by people near and far.

Now share the joy and the love in your heart with all the creatures of the forest. Let them partake of the beauty of your inner vision, letting them feel that there is togetherness in this creation.

Let the joy and love from your heart flow out to nature around you, the flowers, bushes, the trees. With the beauty of your inner vision, the joy and love from your heart flows out to all that surrounds you as part of the same creation.

Match the beauty of your inner vision of the night sky with the moon and stars, with the night sky around you. Enjoy the beauty without and within and love it with your whole heart.

Now put your attention back on yourself. And let the joyfulness and the love that is in your heart fill you from head to toe, surround you, embrace you, and protect you.

May people everywhere have love and joy in their hearts.

## 2. Loving the Breath and Cherishing Life

Please put your attention on the breath for just a few moments. Let a feeling of love arise in your heart for your breath, which is the foundation of your life.

Give your breath the warmth of love and cherish the life energy within your experience, the warmth that you feel in your body, the pulsing, the awareness. Cherish all of it and give it your love.

Put your attention on a person near you. Cherish that person's life energy, the breath that keeps them alive, the warmth of their body, their awareness. Cherish all of that. They are the physical means of our enlightenment.

Think of your parents and cherish them, if they are alive. Think of them in that form, loving the life energy within them. If they are no longer alive, think of them in the form they used to have.

Think of the people who are nearest and dearest to you. Love them and cherish them because they are alive. Love their breath, because it keeps them alive. Love the life energy within them.

Now think of all your friends, let them arise before your mind's eye and love them and cherish them, because they are alive, because they are your friends. Love their life energy. Be aware that that is the means to practice, to grow.

Now think of other people you know. Anyone you would like to think about, close at hand or far away. Cherish and love their life, their breath, their awareness.

Think of the people around you. Let them feel your love. Let them feel that you cherish their lives. And go further afield to people that you might know, have seen, have met, or just heard about. Think of all these people in a way that you can truly feel connected and together, cherishing life as an experience. Give them all your love for no other reason than that they are there to be loved.

Think of the creatures in the forest, large and small—the tiniest ones, like the ant, the bigger ones like the deer, and everything in between—and love and cherish them for being alive, each being a part of the same creation.

And now extend your love to nature around you. Cherish it and love the life energy that is within it.

Put your attention back on yourself and feel the love and the cherishing for yourself as being part of this whole creation. Love the breath, the foundation of life, the warmth of the body, the awareness of the mind— all part of this creation. Feel your love flowing from your heart, filling you from head to toe.

May all beings love and cherish life.

## 3. Breathing In Peace, Breathing Out Love

On your next in-breath fill yourself with peace wherever you think it might come from: the night sky, the trees, the sun, or the wind. Breathe in peace and fill yourself with it. And on your next out-breath breathe out love and surround yourself with it, holding you in a warm embrace. Breathe in peace, fill yourself with it; breathe out love and surround yourself with it.

Now breathe out love and peace to the person sitting next to you. Give that person the greatest gift that you can give, filling him or her with all the peace that you can muster, and surrounding and embracing him or her with all the love that comes from your heart. And as you breathe in and out, fill yourself with more peace and breathe out more love, so that you can give more out of the fullness of your heart.

Now think of your parents, whether they are still alive or not. Breathe out love and peace to them, filling them with all the peace that you can find in yourself, and embrace them with all the love that comes from your heart. And as you breathe in and out, breathe in more peace, breathe out more love. The more love we give, the more love we have within.

Think of those people who are nearest and dearest to you and breathe out love and peace to them. Give the gift of your loving and peaceful heart. Think of your good friends and breathe out love and peace to them. Fill them with all the peace that you can find in yourself as a gift from you and embrace them with all the love you can find in yourself, as a gift from your heart.

Think of those people who are companions in your daily life and breathe out love and peace to them. Let each of them have the gift of your heart, the best gift we can give to anyone.

If you know anyone who is sick or not feeling well, or anyone that is old and not very well, think of them and breathe out love and peace to that person.

If you know anyone who has a lot of grief at this time, breathe out love and peace to that person. If you do not know any such person, think of the people who have a lot of sorrow having lost a loved one, being ill, having bad fortune. Breathe out love and peace to as many of them as you can.

Think of a difficult person whom you know, or any difficult person that you can think of, whom you might not even know personally. Then breathe out the warmth of your love and the calm of your peace to that person, filling him or her with peace, embracing him or her with love. Recognize the dukkha in that person, which makes it easier to love that person.

Breathe out love and peace into your surroundings, knowing that when you do that you are adding to the love and the peace in the world. Let love and peace from your heart reach out into your environment to all sentient beings, to nature, and to the night sky—reach out as far and as wide as the strength of your heart will allow.

And now on your next in-breath breathe in peace and fill yourself with it, and on your next out-breath breathe out love and embrace yourself with it. And do that for the next few minutes as you breathe in and out.

Feel the peace settling in your heart and the love surrounding you like a golden mantle. Anchor both of them in your heart so that you have easy access to them.

May people everywhere have love and peace in their hearts.

## 4. Entering Into the Beauty of the Heart

Please put your attention on the breath for just a few moments.

Use your own creativity to bring about something very beautiful. Decide how best to go about it and then proceed doing that within your own heart. Do you want to fill it with jewels, shining and bright, colorful, translucent, or do you want to fill it with gold, or with flowers?

Fill your heart with the most beautiful aspects you can think of, making it a wonderful place to rest in, and then look at the beauty in your heart, enjoy and love it.

Now let the person sitting nearest to you enter your heart, to enjoy its beauty, to become imbued with the love for that beauty, feeling restful, at ease, and wanting to stay in this beautiful place of your heart.

Now let your parents enter into this beautiful, shining, translucent heart, where they can enjoy, feel loved, and be at rest.

Let your dearest people come into your heart. See how they enjoy and love it, how they appreciate the beauty of it, and how they want to stay there and rest within that beauty.

Now think of your good friends and let them all enter into your heart; see how they smile and appreciate the beauty of your heart. They are happy that they have been allowed to be with you, to enjoy your love, and to find a home in your heart.

Think of the people whom you meet in your everyday life. Take each one by the hand and lead them to your heart. Let them enter and see their enjoyment and their love of this wondrous place, filled with the utmost beauty.

Think of other people you know whom you can lead to your heart. Let them enter and enjoy and be overwhelmed with the beauty they find and the love they experience.

See how your heart is full of people and there is still lots of room for more. There is no limit. The beauty of the heart is limitless. Now think of some people toward whom you are quite indifferent. You neither like nor dislike them. Take them by the hand, let them enter into your heart, see the joy on their faces when they recognize the beauty and the love that they find there.

Now think of some difficult person or persons and recognize the dukkha of that person, take him or her by the hand and lead them to your heart. The beauty and the wonder create real happiness for that person, and you no longer find him or her difficult.

Think of those people whose lives are far more difficult than ours: who may be in a hospital, prison, refugee camp, war zone; or who may be crippled, blind, hungry, without shelter, without friends. Think of the many people that this applies to and take as many of them as you can by the hand and lead them to the beautiful heart that is within you, where they can find joy, and love, and a home. As you lead them to your heart, you can embrace them, so that they know they are really welcome.

Think of the many people who live on this globe of ours, and see whether you can accommodate them all, so that they can all enjoy the wondrous beauty that you have created in your heart, making them happy, making them feel the warmth of love.

Now put your attention back on yourself. Look at the wonderful jewels, or flowers, or the gold of your heart, see how it has created such beauty that when you rest in it, there is joy, and love and peace within you. Think of the joy and the love and the peace as the most wonderful jewels of your heart shining in all directions.

May people everywhere create great beauty in their hearts.

# Notes

1. *The Long Discourses of the Buddha: A Translation of the Dīgha Nikāya,* trans. Maurice Walshe (Boston: Wisdom Publications, 1995). All quotations of the Buddha's words are from this translation, and when not found in the *Poṭṭhapāda Sutta,* are taken from *Suttas* 1 and 2 of the same volume.

2. Described fully in my book *When the Iron Eagle Flies,* published by Penguin, Arkana Division, London, 1991.

3. *The Path of Purification,* translated from the Pali by Ven. Ñāṇnamoli (Kandy, Sri Lanka: The Buddhist Publication Society, 1991).

4. *Majjhima* Commentary, see *The Long Discourses of the Buddha* (see note 1 above), p.555, footnote 224.

# Glossary

The following Pali words encompass concepts and levels of ideas for which there are no adequate synonyms in English. The explanations of these terms have been adapted from *The Buddhist Dictionary* by Nyanatiloka Mahathera.

*Abhiññā*—Five mundane and one supermundane power. The latter is the extinction of all underlying tendencies of greed and hate.

*Abhisaññānirodha*—Higher Extinction of Consciousness (Perception).

*Anāgāmī*—The "Non-Returner" is a noble disciple at the third stage of holiness.

*Ānāpānasati*—Mindfulness of in-breath and out-breath.

*Anattā*—"No-self," non-ego, egolessness, impersonality; "neither within the bodily and mental phenomena of existence, nor outside of them can be found anything that in the ultimate sense could be regarded as a self-existing real ego-identity, soul or any other abiding substance."

*Anicca*—"Impermanence," a basic feature of all conditioned phenomena, be they material or mental, coarse or subtle, one's own or external.

*Arahat/Arahant*—The "Holy One." Through the extinction of all cankers, he reaches already in this very life the deliverance of mind, the deliverance through wisdom, which is free from cankers, and which he himself has understood and realized.

*Ariyā*—Noble Ones. Noble Persons.

*Ariyā iddhi*—The power of controlling one's mind to remain imperturbable, without craving or aversion.

*Arūpa*—Formless spheres.

*Brahmā*—Heavenly beings of the highest order.

*Citta*—Mind, consciousness.

*Dāna*—Generosity.

*Devas*—"Heavenly Beings," deities, celestials are beings who live in happy worlds but are not freed from the cycle of existence.

*Dhamma*—The liberating "law" discovered and proclaimed by the Buddha, summed up in the Four Noble Truths.

*Dhammacakka*—The wheel of Dhamma (of the Law).

*Dukkha*—(1) In common usage: "pain," "painful feeling," which may be bodily or mental. (2) In Buddhist usage as in the Four Noble Truths: suffering, illness, the unsatisfactory nature and general insecurity of all conditioned phenomena.

*Jhāna*—Meditative absorptions. Tranquility meditation.

*Kamma/Karma*— "Action" denotes the wholesome and unwholesome volitions and their concomitant mental factors, causing rebirth and shaping the character of beings and thereby their destiny. The term does not signify the result of actions and most certainly not the deterministic fate of humans.

*Kāma-loka*—The world of the five senses.

*Kasiṇa*—A colored disk, to provide a mental image as a means for concentration.

*Khandha*—The five "groups" are called the five aspects in which the Buddha has summed up all the physical and mental phenomena of existence, and which appear to the ordinary man as his ego or personality, to wit: body, feeling, perception, mental formations, and consciousness.

*Magga-phala*—"Path and fruit." First arises the path-consciousness, immediately followed by "fruition," a moment of supermundane awareness.

*Māra*—The Buddhist "tempter" figure, the personification of evil and passions, of the totality of worldly existence and of death.

*Metta*—"Loving-kindness," one of the four sublime emotions.

*Nibbāna*—Literally "extinction," to cease blowing, to become extinguished. Nibbāna constitutes the highest and ultimate goal of all Buddhist aspirations, i.e., absolute extinction of that life-affirming will manifested as greed, hate, delusion, and clinging to existence, thereby the absolute deliverance from all future rebirth.

*Nirodha*—Extinction (of feeling and perception).

*Pāmojja*—Joy.

*Paññā*—Wisdom (insight).

*Papañca*—"Proliferation," literally "expansion, diffuseness," detailed exposition, development, manifoldness, multiplicity, differentiation.

*Pavadana*—Set rolling (established).

*Puthujjana*—Literally "one of the many folk," worldling, ordinary man, anyone still possessed of all the ten fetters binding to the round of rebirths.

*Rūpa*—Corporeality (in connection with jhāna = fine material).

*Sakadāgāmī*—The "once-returner," having shed the five lower fetters, reappears in a higher world to reach Nibbāna.

*Samatha* —"Tranquility," serenity, is a synonym of *samādhi* (concentration).

*Sampajañña*—Clear comprehension (clarity of consciousness).

*Saṃsāra* —"Round of rebirth," literally "perpetual wandering," is a name designating the sea of life, ever restlessly heaving up and down.

*Sangha*—Literally "congregation," the name for the community of monks and nuns. As the third of the Three Gems and the Three Refuges, it applies to the community of the Noble Ones.

*Sati*—"Mindfulness," the seventh step on the Noble Eightfold Path. The first of the seven factors of enlightenment.

*Sīla*—Morality.

*Sotāpanna*—"Stream-enterer," the first attainment of a noble disciple.

*Sotāpatti*—"Stream-entry," the first attainment of becoming a Noble One.

*Sukha*—"Meditative Happiness," a feature of the first and second meditative absorptions.

*Sutta*—"Discourse" by the Buddha or one of his enlightened disciples.

*Tipiṭaka*—The Three Baskets, a name for the three divisions of the Pali Canon.

*Tathāgata*—The "Perfect One." Literally the one who has thus gone.

*Vicāra*—Sustained application to the meditation subject.

*Vitakka*—Initial application to the meditation subject.

*Vipassanā*—"Insight" into the truth of the impermanence, suffering, and impersonality of all corporal and mental phenomena of existence.

# About the Author

Ayya Khema was born in Berlin in 1923 to Jewish parents. In 1938 she escaped from Germany with a transport of two hundred other children and was taken to Glasgow, Scotland. Her parents went to China and, two years later, Ayya Khema joined them in Shanghai. With the outbreak of war, however, the family was put into a Japanese prisoner-of-war camp and it was here that her father died. She later married, had a son and daughter, and now has four grandchildren.

Four years after the American liberation of the camp, Ayya Khema was able to emigrate to the United States. Between 1960 and 1964 she traveled with her husband and son throughout Asia, including the Himalayan countries, and it was at this time that she learned meditation. Ten years later she began to teach meditation throughout Europe, America, and Australia. Her experiences led her to become ordained as a Buddhist nun in Sri Lanka in 1979, when she was given the name of 'Khema' ('Ayya' means 'Venerable'), meaning safety and security.

She established Wat Buddha Dhamma, a forest monastery in the Theravada tradition, near Sydney, Australia, in 1978. In Colombo she set up the International Buddhist Women's Centre as a training center for Sri Lankan nuns, and Parappuduwa Nun's Island for women who want to practice intensively and/or ordain as nuns. She is the spiritual director of Buddha-Haus in Germany, established in 1989 under her auspices. In June 1997 "Metta Vihara," the first Buddhist forest monastery in Germany, was inaugurated by her, and the first ordinations in the German language took place there.

In 1987 she co-ordinated the first international conference of Buddhist nuns in the history of Buddhism, which resulted in the setting-up of Sakyadhita, a world-wide Buddhist women's organization. H.H. the Dalai Lama was the keynote speaker at the conference. In May 1987, as an invited lecturer, she was the first ever to address the United Nations in New York on the topic of Buddhism.

Ayya Khema has written twenty-five books on meditation and the Buddha's teaching in English and German; her books have been translated into seven languages. In 1988, her book *Being Nobody, Going Nowhere* received the Christmas Humphreys Memorial Award.

# Wisdom Publications

Wisdom Publications, a not-for-profit publisher, is dedicated to making available authentic Buddhist works for the benefit of all. We publish translations of the sutras and tantras, commentaries and teachings of past and contemporary Buddhist masters, and original works by the world's leading Buddhist scholars. We publish our titles with the appreciation of Buddhism as a living philosophy and with the special commitment to preserve and transmit important works from all the major Buddhist traditions.

If you would like more information or a copy of our mail order catalogue, please write to us at:

WISDOM PUBLICATIONS
199 Elm Street
Somerville, Massachusetts 02144
USA

# The Wisdom Trust

As a not-for-profit publisher, Wisdom Publications is dedicated to the publication of fine Dharma books for the benefit of all sentient beings and dependent upon the kindness and generosity of sponsors in order to do so. If you would like to make a donation to Wisdom, please contact our Somerville office.

Thank you.

*Wisdom Publications is a non-profit, charitable 501 (c)(3) organization and a part of the Foundation for the Preservation of the Mahayana Tradition (FPMT).*

# Also Available from Wisdom Publications

For orders call (800) 272-4050

---

**Being Nobody, Going Nowhere: Meditations on the Buddhist Path**
Ayya Khema
192 pages, 0-86171-052-5, $12.95

In this book Ayya Khema gives clear, practical instructions on meditation and techniques for overcoming conditioned mental habits, ideas, beliefs, and limiting thinking patterns. She also includes an eloquent outline of the Buddhist path that can be understood and enjoyed by everybody.

"This book is a valuable guide to the path of meditative insight and loving compassion. It is direct, clear, and inspiring." —Sharon Salzberg, author of *Lovingkindness*

"Not just highly recommended but essential reading for hearts inclined to the path."—*DharmaCrafts*

**Great Disciples of the Buddha: Their Lives, Their Works, Their Legacy**
Nyanaponika Thera and Hellmuth Hecker
Edited with an Introduction by Bhikkhu Bodhi
448 pages, 0-86171-128-9, $29.95

A unique collection of biographies of extraordinary men and women who attained great spiritual realizations under the direct guidance of the Buddha 2500 years ago.

"I am grateful for the publication of this book...I recommend *Great Disciples* to friends and students alike."—Thich Nhat Hanh, author of *Living Buddha, Living Christ*

"A truly excellent and unique new edition to the literature from the Pali texts."—Jack Kornfield, author of *A Path with Heart*

**The Middle Length Discourses of the Buddha: A New Translation of the Majjhima Nikaya**
Translated by Bhikkhu Ñanamoli & Bhikkhu Bodhi
1424 pages, 0-86171-072-X, $60.00

*1995 Outstanding Academic Book Award —Choice Magazine*
*Tricycle Prize for Excellence in Buddhist Publishing for "Dharma Discourse"*

The 152 discourses of this major collection combine a rich variety of contextual settings with deep and comprehensive teachings.

"...remarkable both in its scope and in its contemporary rendering of the Buddha's words."—*Tricycle: The Buddhist Review*

**The Long Discourses of the Buddha: A Translation of the Digha Nikaya**
Translated by Maurice Walshe
656 pages, 0-86171-103-3, $34.95

An invaluable collection of the teachings of the Buddha, which reveal his gentleness, compassion, and penetrating wisdom. These thirty-four discourses are among the oldest records of the Buddha's original teachings. (Previously titled *Thus Have I Heard*)